Primary Teacher's Handbook

2nd Edition

Also available from Continuum

Primary Teacher's Handbook

2nd Edition

Lyn Overall and Margaret Sangster

continuum

Continuum International Publishing Group
The Tower Building   80 Maiden Lane, Suite 704
11 York Road   New York, NY 10038
London SE1 7NX

www.continuumbooks.com

British Library Cataloguing-in-Publication Data
A catalogue record for this book is available from the British Library.

ISBN: 978 0 82649 343 9 (paperback)

Typeset by Acorn Bookwork Ltd
Printed and bound in Great Britain by MPG Books Ltd

Contents

Introduction

This book is about working on becoming a more effective teacher through a process of evaluation and action.

> Outstanding teachers continuously set and meet ambitious targets for themselves and their pupils. They refer regularly to visible, quantifiable and tangible measures; and they focus on whether they and the school are making a difference and adding value to pupils.
>
> (Hay McBer, 2000:1.3.9)

When effective teachers talk about how they work it is hard for them to express the complexity of decision making which occurs from minute to minute in managing a class. Success is a mixture of hard work, knowledge, personality, professional commitment and the implementation of a range of teaching skills. Professional knowledge and teaching skills are acquired and refined over many years. This book offers an analytical reflection on teaching strategies and a model for implementation of those strategies. From our experience of observing teachers and students at work, we feel that the self-evaluation process is one of the most effective ways to develop teaching skills. In England this idea is embedded in the Standards framework (TDA, January 2007 Draft).

Teaching is one of those professions in which it is difficult to feel you know enough to cope with everything that comes your way. There always seem to be new situations to deal with; a pupil who tests all your current strategies and patience; a new initiative to introduce; a new technology to assimilate. The feeling of 'I need to know more' never goes away throughout your career. In our ever-changing society, it would not be too extreme to say, that we have come to accept an element of continuous development in most professional work.

As a student in training, the learning curve is steep and initially driven by survival! Gradually the focus moves away from yourself to questions about pupils' learning and the effectiveness of the strategies you are using. Students who learn most rapidly are those who reflect on their own development and take action to improve their teaching. You may identify areas which need development and set your own targets on which to work. The class teacher and the mentor will help you with this. This book is written to support target-setting.

There is an expectation that teachers will continue to develop their skills and qualifications and an indication that teachers will, in future, track their own professional development in a profile document. This already happens with newly qualified teachers (TTA, 1998). As a teacher you may choose to further develop your teaching strategies and will find the contents of this book a useful starting point.

Teachers are not the only adults who work with children in school. Teaching assistants are placed in charge of a group or work with individuals. They are faced with similar situations to the class teacher. The strategies employed to deal with these situations will, on many occasions, be the same as those used by the teacher. Within these pages there are suggestions which will support the management of groups and individuals.

Within the book there is information on aspects of teaching, suggested teaching strategies and reference to where you can obtain further information on topics. The revision of this book takes place at a time of change. In the first edition entries are mapped to official documentation about teacher training in England (DfES/TTA, 2002). This mapping is available in the Appendix. In this edition the mapping is against the *Professional Standards for Teachers* (TDA, January 2007 Draft). This mapping and framework is available in the Appendix.

Although the entries can be used purely as reference material, their main contribution will be as a practical support to developing teaching strategies in the classroom. Part One outlines how the teaching strategies can be developed as part of the process of self-evaluation. This is followed in Part Two by an A–Z of topics which promote the development of effective teaching strategies. Each entry has a first section to help you think about what is involved in the topic. Links are then made with other relevant topics in the book. This is followed by bullet-pointed strategies for you to select as targets. An additional section offers further discussion on each topic. There are also some suggestions for further reading.

Further reading

Department for Education and Skills/Teacher Training Agency (2002) *Qualifying to Teach, Professional Standards for Qualified Teacher Status and Requirements for Initial Teacher Training*, London: TTA Publication no. TPU 0803/02-02 (weblink www.canteach.gov.uk).

Department for Education and Skills/Teacher Development Agency (2007 Draft) *Professional Standards for Teachers in England: Personal Professional Development*, London: TDA.

Hay McBer (2000) *Research into Teacher Effectiveness: A Model of Teacher Effectiveness.* London: Department for Education and Employment (weblink www.dfes.gov.uk/teachingreforms/leadership/mcber).

Teacher Training Agency (1998) *Career Entry Profile for Newly Qualified Teachers*, London: TTA.

www.teachernet.gov.uk has links for all the government papers.

Part One
THE SELF-EVALUATION PROCESS

The self-evaluation process

We have observed over a period of years that the student teachers and teachers who make best use of the evaluation process make good progress in their effectiveness in the classroom. They work on how to manage a classroom and how to provide an effective learning environment for their pupils. The process they use is similar to the assessment process that takes place with pupils in class. It is accepted that assessment is a part of ensuring good pupil progress. Teachers look at pupils' work and comment on their progress against set criteria. This collection and evaluation of data are two steps in the assessment process. The third step is to act upon the results by planning an appropriate next step to take with the pupils. This process is known as formative assessment. It is an invaluable stage in the teaching cycle. It is not enough to say, 'I have planned this, I have taught this and that's my job done.'

Effective teachers respond to the needs of the pupils in their class. They adapt and adjust work so that it builds on pupils' current knowledge. When discovering misconceptions, effective teachers backtrack and re-teach, so that pupils have correct understanding. Assessment allows teachers to recognize where pupils are in their learning and to respond accurately to pupils' needs. This can be described as a *cycle of teaching* which *spirals* forward as assessment informs the next planning.

– teaching – assessing (recording) – planning – teaching – assessing –

In this book we are suggesting that you apply a parallel cycle of self-evaluation and target-setting to your own teaching skills. By *closing the loop* on your own learning by assessing your needs and taking action, you can generate a model that carries the development of your teaching skills forward. You, or a mentor you are working with, identify a target for improvement. You then decide on a strategy to deal with the situation and try it out. Most important of all, you then need to assess whether your strategy was effective and can be used again, or whether you must try another. It is easy to see how this will enable you to build a repertoire of successful strategies for use in your work.

If you are a student teacher this consultation procedure will be part of your training. If you are a teaching assistant this will be part of the process of working with teacher colleagues. If you are a teacher looking to progress through thresholds then this process can be used to provide some of the evidence for your line manager to make judgements about your work. The process that is recommended here will assist student teachers (trainees) and teachers in both reflection and improvement. This is an explicit requirement in the *Framework for Professional Standards for Teachers in England: Personal professional development* (TDA: January 2007 Draft) (Q7(a, b). Trainees and teachers (and teaching assistants in their standards) are required to be reflective about their practice and proactive in improvement.

The process of self-evaluation

The process of self-evaluation has several steps. These lead you through the decision making that is required to solve a problem, meet a challenge or make a minor adjustment to your teaching. The steps are:

1. Identify the cause for your concern – name the issue.
2. Consider the available strategies.
3. Select a strategy.
4. Try it out.
5. Did it work?
6. If yes – keep it in the repertoire.
7. If no – select another strategy and try again.
8. Start again at 1 on the next strategy.

1. Identify the cause for your concern – name the issue

If something is not going well in the classroom you will want to make improvements. If it is a problem, first you have to identify it – naming what you think it is. For example, you note that in your lesson:

- some pupils are getting bored
- there is some poor behaviour
- some able children are disengaging from work and are underperforming.

This combination might have several causes but after some thought about this you decide that your planning and task for the lesson are fine, the problem is that the pace is slow. The slow pace is boring some pupils, giving rise to poor behaviour and less than satisfactory work. It could have been a combination of problems, but this time you decide it is one problem that gives rise to several 'symptoms' that you want to improve.

In this book, if you are sure what is causing the problem you can look up the cause directly. Sometimes you may have to read several sections and follow the links before you find comments that match the situation you are considering.

As the process of identifying the cause to be addressed and naming the issue may take some working out, it is often helpful to discuss the situation with an experienced teacher. They can often pinpoint the main cause and help you to consider appropriate strategies.

2. Consider the available strategies

Once you have identified the area in which you are working, you need to select a strategy. Some possible strategies are offered under each heading. You might feel that one or several of these are appropriate. Reading the commentary and reflecting on the issue could help you to formulate a strategy of your own.

3. Select a strategy

Select the strategy which you think will be most effective in your situation. You may wish to select more than one strategy and trial them simultaneously. Trying out a strategy might involve refining that strategy until it is effective. It might be that you set three targets to work at simultaneously. These may or may not be linked. A linked example would be that you have a child whose behaviour you wish to change and you have three strategies that you are going to try out. In the following example there are three strategies for dealing with a child who can be disruptive:

(i) You are going to ignore interruption during the whole-class 'carpet' session and deal with behaviour at the end.

(ii) You are going to ensure that the child starts on the task by sharing the first few minutes with him.

(iii) You are always going to finish any conversation with the child with a statement of praise about one positive aspect of his work or behaviour.

4. Try it out

Having decided what you are going to do, try it. You may decide to trial your chosen strategy over one or more days.

5. Did it work?

It is important to evaluate the effectiveness of what you chose to do. Sometimes the strategy you've chosen will take time to have an effect. Sometimes it becomes clear quite quickly that the strategy is not the right one for the context. Returning to ask whether it worked or not is part of the conscious process of permanently adopting the strategy or throwing it out.

6. If yes – keep it in the repertoire

If the strategy worked then give yourself a pat on the back and make sure you keep using it for as long as it is appropriate.

7. If no – select another strategy and try again

Not everything is going to work first time. If the strategy does not work it is worth talking to someone about the situation. He/she might have a different view on the cause and can help you think through the possible solutions. It might be that you have selected an appropriate strategy, but it is going to take time to work. Some children can be resistant for the whole year! You might, now you have thought and observed more about the situation, decide that a different strategy is more appropriate.

8. Start again at 1 on the next strategy

If you have been successful you will be ready to work on another problem, challenge or minor adjustment in your teaching, so move on to your next target. If success has eluded you, have a rethink and persevere with the same strategy or select a new one. It is important to sustain the momentum and make the evaluative process part of your normal practice.

A format to support the self-evaluation process

Figure 1 shows a suggested format that allows for three 'visits' to the self-evaluation process. It is followed by two examples of how it can be used in conjunction with this book. Example 1 is drawn from a need identified by a student from her classroom experience. Example 2 is from a teacher seeking to improve an aspect of his work.

Self-evaluation of teaching strategies	
The aspect of teaching or learning I wish to improve	
Strategy to try	Evaluation
	Success / try another strategy
The aspect of teaching or learning I wish to improve	
Strategy to try	Evaluation
	Success / try another strategy
The aspect of teaching or learning I wish to improve	
Strategy to try	Evaluation
	Success / try another strategy

Figure 1   Format to support the self-evaluation process

Example 1: Marie's transitions

Marie, a student teacher, realizes that she is having difficulty moving the class from one place to another. One of the times is when they all finish one activity and have to move to the next, such as moving from the whole-class teaching on the carpet to group activities at the tables. The children are noisy, start to wander round the class, some finding other things to do. She usually ends up raising her voice, stopping everyone and telling them off. Particularly difficult is the time when children finish their work at different times. These periods of time are known as 'transitions'.

Having identified where the problem lies she looks in the A–Z section at *Transitions*. Here she finds that there are several types of transition and several possible causes for them not going smoothly. At this point she needs to select what she is going to work on first. Is it going to be: clearer instructions; a different strategy for getting children to move from one place to another; or a change in the work set? She may wish to take on more than one strategy. The important point is for Marie to identify what is causing the problem. She may be able to discuss this with her class teacher who has been observing her teaching.

Having selected the strategy to try out, Marie then needs to write it on the form.

Self-evaluation of teaching strategies

The aspect of teaching or learning I wish to improve

Transitions

Strategy to try	Evaluation
Clearer end of task instructions *Sending groups one at a time from carpet to tables*	
	Success / try another strategy

At this stage only 'The aspect of teaching or learning I wish to improve' and the 'Strategy to try' sections are completed. At the end of the day Marie returns to the form to do her evaluation and consider her next target.

From the way Marie fills in the evaluation we can see she has had some partial success. She wishes to change one of her strategies slightly and focus again on it. She will maintain the successful strategy of sending them off to work, a group at a time.

Self-evaluation of teaching strategies

The aspect of teaching or learning I wish to improve

Transitions

Strategy to try	Evaluation
Clearer end of task instructions	*I still need to work on this*
Sending groups one at a time from carpet to tables	*This was much better* *I shall keep this*
	Success / try another strategy

The aspect of teaching or learning I wish to improve

Continue with transitions

Strategy to try	Evaluation
Clearer end of task instructions with sitting or lining up place included	
	Success / try another strategy

Example 2: Peter's marking strategies

Peter, a teacher in his second year of teaching has noticed that many of his Year 5 class pay little attention to the marks he gives for maths and English. Currently he operates a system where children receive a mark out of 10 for each piece of work. These he collects in a record book and averages out for the half-term. He occasionally writes a brief phrase such as 'good work', 'satisfactory' or 'see me' on the pupils' books. He would like his pupils to show more concern about errors and improving their performance.

Self-evaluation of teaching strategies	
The aspect of teaching or learning I wish to improve *Pupil engagement in addressing errors*	
Strategy to try *Time slot to discuss errors with peers and whole class*	Evaluation
	Success / try another strategy

On reflection, and having read the sections on marking and feedback, he feels he has two choices; to instigate a more competitive environment or to involve the pupils in reviewing and evaluating their work. He is not sure whether these two strategies are mutually exclusive, but opts to try and promote the second strategy.

Peter decides to begin the next maths lesson with pupils discussing with each other any mistakes they had made. He is aware he might have to pair some children who had 10 out of 10 with those who had made many mistakes.

Peter found that the discussion was useful because the pupils fed back to him that they were now more comfortable with the maths. This was a gain, but the start of the session was very ragged and much time was taken. Peter therefore decided to adjust his strategy to make it more structured. He was not sure whether this would increase or decrease pupil understanding, but was prepared to seek further feedback from pupils.

Self-evaluation of teaching strategies

The aspect of teaching or learning I wish to improve

Pupil engagement in addressing errors

Strategy to try	Evaluation
Time slot to discuss errors with peers and whole class	*Peer discussion took longer than expected but pupils were clearer about where they had gone wrong*
	Whole class discussion made it even longer and pupils not forthcoming about mistakes
	Success / try another strategy

The aspect of teaching or learning I wish to improve

Continue with pupil engagement in addressing errors, but reduce time involved

Strategy to try	Evaluation
I will select most common mistake to discuss with whole class to start with,	
then,	Success / try another strategy
5 minute time limit on peer discussion if needed	

While the strategy Peter tried has led to more engagement by the pupils he has now gone on to question how meaningful giving marks out of 10 are and how constructive his comments are to the pupils. He has begun to examine further his assessment and feedback strategies.

Further uses of evaluation strategies and target-setting in teaching

In Part Two, the entries which are most directly about teaching, include suggested strategies which are written in the present tense, in an instructional form. This is for use when carrying out the strategy in the classroom. For example, 'Allow 10 minutes for a plenary', 'Check the clock every 10 minutes to see if I am on schedule'. By changing the form to a question it can also be used as a check when planning. For example, 'Have I allowed time for a plenary?' When evaluating the success of your strategy you will move into question mode again. For example, 'Did I allow time for the plenary? Did I check the clock?'

Self-evaluation is a powerful process. Here we are recommending you use it on your teaching skills. The same procedure can also be used in evaluating the effectiveness of a lesson. Did the lesson meet the objective? If yes, well done and move on. If no, then what shall I change next time?

It is also useful to use the process with individual pupils. For example, if you have a shy child you can consider what strategy you can use to encourage him/her to join in group discussion. At the end of the week you can assess whether your strategy has been effective. This could be recorded in the pupils' ongoing profile. As well as being a proactive way of working with children it also helps you to be consistent in your responses, which sends clear messages about behaviour to the children in your class.

International perspectives

This book is mostly about generic teaching skills. The strategies suggested will apply to many contexts. In countries where students training to be teachers are required to meet criteria or competencies or professional standards, entries can be 'mapped' against these. These could be integrated into the target-setting and recorded in the official profile. In England, to qualify to teach, statutory requirements have to be met (TDA, January 2007 Draft). Where they apply, we have mapped entries against these TDA 2007 requirements, appending the 2002 requirements in the Appendix. Some of the information-giving entries are about primary education in England, while some are of general application.

A note on terminology

Words mean different things in different countries. This book uses English terms. We write about our school-age learners as children, pupils or students. In the USA and Canada, learners of all ages are students. In the USA, Canada and in some South American countries grades equate to chronological age but progression to the next grade is based on competence. In the rest of the world children are usually grouped by chronological age and progress with advancing age. In England, most children enter schooling before they are five, some start nursery education when they are three. The five year olds go into a Reception class. At six they progress to a Year 1 class, which normally equates to Grade 1 in most of the USA, and to Primary 2 in Scotland. In the UK, children are in primary school until the age of 11. These are known as elementary schools in Canada and the USA. Eleven to 18 year olds in the UK go to secondary school, in North America, Australia and New Zealand these students attend high school.

In the UK education system, central government determines much of the structure and provision for education. For example, in England there is a National Curriculum with Key Stage tests at seven, 11 and 16. There are also national qualifications, usually by public examination, at end stages of secondary education. And there is a national inspection system. Wales, Scotland and Northern Ireland have their own systems.

In England, while funding is increasingly channelled directly into schools, local government in the form of local authorities (LAs) also allocate funds from local and central taxation. This has reduced the role of the local authority education department. Contrast this with North America, where diversity is considerable as education is a district and state responsibility. Some states have an outline curriculum and take part in some national examinations for older students, but it is not possible to generalize.

Terminology varies in internal matters too. For example, in English schools the senior manager is usually known as the headteacher, while in North America, the senior manager in school is the school principal. In the UK free time between lessons is known as break; while it is called recess in North America. School work in the UK is marked; in the USA it is graded.

Further reading

TDA, January 2007 Draft at www.tda.gov.uk/upload/resources/pdf/d/draft_revised_standards_framework_
jan_2007.pdf

References

Q7(a, b), Q8, Q9, Q29.

Part Two
A–Z OF EFFECTIVE TEACHING STRATEGIES

Able children

Often able children are talented in many aspects of school work. Occasionally a child has a talent in one specific area such as music, art or mathematics. Able children's cycle of learning has a different balance. There is a quick uptake of new learning with the child making links to his/her prior experience. They need only a short consolidation or practice period, and enjoy applying the learning to new and challenging situations. Problem solving is a good example of one way of meeting able children's needs.

Sometimes able children become withdrawn. Sometimes they get impatient with slower children and prefer to work on their own. As a teacher you have to find the balance between developing all aspects of the child, including working with others. You need to create opportunities which let the child stretch his/her abilities.

Some children are educationally advanced because they are more mature, have received rich educational experiences at home or have been coached in a subject. It is the teacher's task to work out what each child is capable of and provide a suitably challenging curriculum.

Links

Differentiation
Expectations about pupils' learning
Group work
Problem solving

Strategies

- Increase an able pupil's decision-making opportunities.
- Lessen practice time and increase time spent on application of knowledge.
- Try presenting work initially as a problem.
- Adjust the group task so it is more challenging for the able child.
- Try to find times when able children work with you and with other able children.

Development

Much has been written about able children and gifted children. It is recognized that children can be talented at different things. Gardner (1983) theorizes that multiple intelligences exist and the brain develops with strengths in a possible seven areas, such as spatial intelligence, music intelligence and numerical intelligence. It is generally recognised that Intelligence Quotient

(IQ) tests are a rather general way of measuring ability and it is more effective to deal with specific abilities. This is not easy when teaching classes of 30 children. When trying to establish what able children know, it appears they can do all the things you ask of them within the normal range of the curriculum for your year group. It is probable that they can do half the work before you teach them so it is understandable that they get bored. It is vital that they engage in new learning. This may mean that you have to cater for their needs on an individual basis.

Alongside the academic needs of the able child, the teacher needs to ensure that social development and good working practices are addressed. It is very easy to isolate able children. They get impatient when working with children who think at a slower rate than them. They get fed up acting as a surrogate teacher. Other children can treat them as 'different' and find them threatening. They can easily get used to working on their own and some find it slow and tedious to articulate their thinking. A variety of approaches and experiences needs to be utilized, appropriate to the expected outcomes of the task. Muijs and Reynolds (2001) offer a good account of the needs and organization of gifted children in the classroom.

Further reading

Gardner, H. (1983) *Frames of Mind: A Theory of Multiple Intelligences*, London: Heinemann.

Muijs, D. and Reynolds, D. (2001) *Effective Teaching: Evidence and Practice*, London: Paul Chapman Publishing.

TDA references

Q15, Q16.

Active learning

How can we put children in a position to control their own learning? To be active learners they need to be able to

- forecast how well they will do on various tasks
- know what they already understand about the tasks
- know what aspects of the tasks they can do.

Active learners can transfer what they know to new tasks. In a modern society active learning is important because individuals will need to be able to do new things as new challenges arise. Our responsibility is to enable children to reflect on and improve their own abilities to learn. There are three important ideas that underpin active learning: formative assessment; thorough teaching; and teaching children how to learn.

Open formative assessment Children come to our schools knowing many things. We have to know and use what each of them understands about what they are learning. This has implications for assessment. In the model of active learning it is not sufficient to test at end points. Assessment has to be a continuous monitoring of knowledge and understanding. Constructive and supportive feedback helps to make explicit to the individual what he/she knows and what still has to be learned. It is a way of modelling the process of reflective learning.

Teach less, more thoroughly Coverage of the curriculum is important but we don't have to teach everything all at once. Trying to cover everything means that much of what is taught is without depth. Knowledge, concepts and skills can be carefully managed to ensure coverage during the school years. However, this is not to deny the importance of completeness in any subject. Rather it suggests that an in-depth understanding of subject concepts and factual knowledge is more important than superficial coverage of the whole discipline. You'll know that bits of the subjects you teach can be hard to grasp. Your job is to make learning 'the hard to grasp bit' possible. You'll do this by giving an overview, 'This is what we are learning'. Breaking the learning into small steps and relating these back to what children are learning. It helps to use a great many examples about one concept. It is important that the children find the learning as easy as possible. As some children are resistant to challenge, it is important to avoid indicating that what they are doing is hard to learn. You will want to be encouraging, 'You are working hard', while they are learning. You will want to celebrate success by telling them, 'You're clever at this now'. End-point assessment should test children's deep understanding rather than their surface knowledge. This also ensures public accountability.

Taking time to ensure that children's factual knowledge is accurate and secure is very important. To do this your own understanding of factual knowledge and the concepts of the subjects you teach and their disciplines (ways of working and thinking) are crucial. Of equal importance is your knowledge about how children learn each subject. As a teacher both are prerequisites for the children in your class to be active learners.

Teach children how to learn This means the internal dialogue that goes on when anyone learns anything is important. Making this explicit to your children is really important. They need to know that talking about what they are learning is part of the learning process. They need to know that 'talking in the head' (metacognition) is part of the learning process. Working in pairs and small groups to solve particular problems is a powerful way of modelling this. You need to be able to help them know how subjects work; you'll want to explore with them all the things that make each distinctive, for example, the language of the topic, its concepts, theory, philosophy, processes and procedures.

Links

Feedback
Formative assessment
Independent learning
Learning styles
Recording individual progress
Self-assessment by pupils
Subject knowledge
Summative assessment
Thinking skills

Strategies

To enable active learning:

Before beginning a new topic:

- check what each child knows about the topic
- know the common preconceptions and possible misconceptions about the topic.

In your preparation ensure that you:

- are providing factually accurate knowledge
- understand the facts and ideas within a conceptual framework
- know which areas might be hard to learn
- organize what you teach to make it easy to recall and use.

In each session:

- clearly define learning goals with the children
- use small steps and really carefully chosen examples to make the 'hard to grasp' easy to learn

- keep checking what has been understood
- tell children what they have learned about the topic
- tell them what else they need to do to learn about the topic
- tell children about the ways in which they have been successful as learners
- give them something more to work on to be even more successful learners.

Development

The term active learning can be misleading, as it has overtones of frantic behaviour. The term 'engaged learning' may be preferable. The engaged learner may not exhibit any outward signs of activity. Critical thinking is not that easily observed. Our understanding about active learning for children is based on a science of learning. Each of these headings provides its theoretical underpinning. They are starting places for developing a deeper understanding about active learning.

a. Memory and the structure of knowledge.
b. Problem solving and reasoning.
c. Early foundations of learning.
d. Regulatory processes that govern learning (including metacognition). This is about how the brain learns.
e. Symbolic thinking and culture and learning community.

Further reading

National Research Council (2000) *How People Learn*, Washington: National Academic Press. Seminal US report that used extensive review of available research to make statements about learning and teaching.

Pollard, A. with Collins, J., Maddock, M., Simco, N., Swaffield, S., Warin, J. and Warwick, P. (2002) *Reflective Teaching* (2nd edn): *Evidence-informed Professional Practice*, London: Continuum. Chapter 7 is informative and the suggested additional readings make this a most useful text.

Sousa, D. A. (2001) *How the Brain Learns: A Classroom Teacher's Guide* (2nd edn), Thousand Oaks: Corwin. This is a really practical guide on how to improve your teaching and children's learning through understanding how the brain works.

Whitehead, D. (ed.) (2000) *The Psychology of Teaching and Learning in the Primary School*, London: Routledge/Falmer. Section II: 'Teaching the Curriculum' is a starting place for exploring these ideas.

TDA reference

Q10.

Assessment

See entries: *Feedback, Formative assessment, Self-assessment by pupils, Summative assessment.*

Behaviour

See *Discipline.*

Bullying

It is useful to think of bullying or harassment as a particular type of aggressive behaviour. The bully intends to hurt the victim. The hurt can be physical or psychological or both. When children open up about this they emphasize the effects of bullying. There is no doubt that victims get extremely distressed. Bullying is generally thought to have three characteristics:

- It is unprovoked.
- It occurs repeatedly.
- The bully is stronger, or thought to be stronger, than the victim.

Bullying is repeated action; a one-off incident, while unpleasant, isn't bullying. More than once is enough to take serious action. Usually bullying takes these forms:

- *physical aggression* – being hit
- *verbal aggression* – name calling
- *indirect* – being ignored, left out, nasty looks.

Anyone, or any group, who finds that he/she/they can get a response by using aggression, can bully. Often the bully will have a gang who support tacitly, if not actively. It is difficult to detect, as bullying doesn't go on in the teacher's sight. Most bullying in school is well hidden and disguised. Most bullies will vehemently deny involvement in bullying. While obvious victims are children who are different, either physically, emotionally or intellectually, unfortunately, if the circumstances are right, any child can be a victim. Some English research has suggested that 1 in 4 children of primary age are bullied more than once or twice in any one term (Smith, Pepler and Rigby, 2004). Bullied children may be very reluctant to tell. Victims may blame themselves, they quickly lose self-confidence and self-esteem. They will find it difficult to concentrate. Some will take time off from school to avoid being bullied. They may achieve less well than predicted.

nt for signs of bullying; they should always investigate suspected inci-
s promptly. Parents and carers need to be involved at an early stage.
achieve change, a problem-solving approach, working with both victim
l bully to make the situation clear, can often work. It is your job to
low up on all incidents, to make sure that bullying is not resumed.

Further reading

Smith, P. K., Pepler, D. and Rigby, K. (2004) *Bullying in Schools: How Successful Can Interventions Be?*, Cambridge: Cambridge University Press.

Bullying: Don't Suffer in Silence; An anti-bullying pack for schools can be downloaded from www.teachernet.gov.uk/wholeschool/behaviour/tacklingbullying/antibullyingpack

www.circle-time.co.uk Jenny Mosely's site for all aspects of dealing with bullying.

www.bullying.co.uk

www.scre.ac.uk/bully.

TDA references

Q3(a, b), Q18, Q21(a, b) Q30, Q31.

Challenge

See *Child development, Expectations about pupils' learning.*

Child development

Some aspects of development are obvious. As you look at children in the playground you spot that younger children are not as physically developed as older children. The questions teachers need to answer are about when and how children acquire all sorts of skills and knowledge. There are many models about development. Some models assume that change is continuous. In these there is an expectation that all seven year olds will be able to, for example, skip. Development is continuous, gradual and inevitable, it is orderly and smooth. Discontinuous development would suggest that there is a stage when everything is in place for the child to be able to skip. This view sees development as ragged and uneven. In the example, children would learn to skip if all those things that enable skipping to happen were in place: wanting to skip, having someone to help, as well as all the other physical attributes such as balance, skeletal strength and muscle development. It might hold that most seven year olds will be able to skip, but some children

Links

Child protection
Communication about learning
Communication with parents
Discipline
Emotional development
Equal opportunities
Purposeful working atmosphere
Social development
Values and ethos

Strategies

This has to be dealt with through a whole-school approach; par
carers, all the adults in the school and all the children need to be in
It should be a high priority. In the school:

- Everyone should know what bullying is and what to do if they become aware it is happening.
- Monitoring of bullying should be going on. Anonymous questionnaires are an effective means of collecting this data.
- Free time, between lessons and in the school grounds, needs active supervision, with a range of activities to keep children happily engaged and a support network for children who experience bullying.
- Displaying helpline posters will help children who find it most difficult to tell.
- All children will be encouraged to take positive action against bullying.

In your classroom prevention should be the key, teach how to:

- Build cooperative relationships with other children through group activities and a variety of pairings, etc.
- Resist bullying behaviour through role play, peer discussion, the choice of stories to be read aloud, etc.
- Develop alternatives to aggression, with the children, as a means of sorting differences through modelling, discussion and role play.

Development

Bullying and harassment can be real barriers to learning. This is one very
good reason to make sure that it is always taken seriously. Teachers need to
encourage children to tell an adult if they are being bullied, or if they know
someone who is being bullied. This means that what bullying is, and what
it isn't, has to be talked about regularly and frequently. Teachers need to be

can skip at a much younger age and others will be much older. All models attempt to account for stability and change. In considering temperament, for example, is an outgoing child always going to be that way (is this stable?) or will the outgoingness change over time (is it unstable?)? Thinkers about development are also interested in the extent to which heritability (what comes from the inherited genes) and environment interact. These questions are about how you make the most of what you are born with.

There may be important periods where some learning is most easily accomplished. If these milestones have been missed, then schooling has to offer the opportunity for catching up. For example, motor skills, learning to walk, run, jump, may be best accomplished in the first six years (see *Physical development*). Young children need to have the opportunity to develop physical skills in school. Emotional control (see *Emotional development*) can be learned after the 'terrible twos' but may need more help right through the years at school. It may be sensible to use the developing brain capacity (see *Intellectual development*) to acquire language from 0–12 years, to include both first and additional language teaching at this age (see *Linguistic development*). It certainly seems to be more difficult to become proficient in an additional language if teaching is delayed until 13. This means that teachers have to take account of individual development to ensure that the teaching and learning are effective.

Links

Emotional development
Intellectual development
Linguistic development
Social development

Further reading

Keenan, T. (2002) *An Introduction to Child Development*, London: Sage. This is an example of many books about development.

Overall, L. S. (2007) *Supporting Children's Learning*, London: Sage. This introductory textbook is about learning and development.

Smith, P. K., Cowie, H. and Blades, M. (2003) *Understanding Children's Development* (4th edn). Oxford: Blackwell. This is an excellent scholarly text on development.

TDA reference

Q18.

Child protection

Child protection is to do with the role that school has in keeping the child safe. In an educational setting, the 'child' will include anyone who is not legally an adult. The *Every Child Matters* agenda has increased awareness about child abuse and reinforced the determination to do something to protect children and young people. Teachers and all those wo work with children have a statutory *duty of care*. The Children Act 1989, since strengthened and reinforced by other law-relating Agenda sets out the key principles:

- The child is a person and not an object of concern.
- Parents and carers are entitled to be treated with greater respect and kept more fully informed.
- Statutory powers should be used only when necessary and last for the minimum time possible.
- Careful consideration should be given to the operation inter-agency procedures.

In the statutory framework:

- The child's welfare is of 'paramount consideration'.
- Delay is likely to be prejudicial to the child and should be avoided.
- Courts should not make care orders unless it is clear that to do so would be better for the child than not doing so.
- Decisions should be made in partnership wherever possible.
- Children have a right to be consulted and listened to when decisions are being made about their lives.

Both the principles and the law are similar in other countries. As in England and Wales, in many other countries the education service is part of the inter-agency approach. This means that teachers act not as individuals but as part of a shared approach. Most teachers are neither qualified nor authorised to sort out child abuse. In England and Wales teachers report to the named person within the school (every school has a designated senior member of staff, often the head). This person receives training for the role.

Categories of abuse/identification

A child is considered to be abused or at risk of abuse by parents or other carers, when the basic needs of the child are not being met through avoidable acts either of commission or omission. This means that a parent or carer may be doing something horrid to the child or may be neglecting to do something, for example, not providing regular food. To make these judgements, knowing what the developmental milestones are is important knowledge for you. You should know the physical and mental stages that children and adolescents go through.

Physical harm

Remember that parenting is very hard work. From time to time parents and carers walk to the edge of a metaphorical cliff, and infuriated beyond control, unfortunately some fall off. Be open-minded, but be vigilant. Not everything is wickedness, but not everything is innocent either.
For example, consider:

- Black eyes – one, occasionally, is an accident, two may be an indication that a child has been hit deliberately, i.e. a non-accidental injury.
- Bruising – the shape of the bruise is important, if you saw eight round bruises on either side of a child's back and two on either side of the ribs it might a game where someone, entirely innocently, throws the child in the air and catches them. But it might be that the child has been shaken.
- Round burns anywhere indicate cigarette burns and, without doubt, are something that should be further investigated.

Neglect/failure to thrive

- For example, consider a pupil who loses weight during a school holiday.

Emotional abuse

- For example, consider the child who is obsessively good in your class. He/she may be in a home environment of low warmth and high criticism and is afraid to get things wrong.

Sexual abuse

- For example, consider a five year old who knows the names of genitals and plays sexy games with dolls or other children. It is really hard to make this judgement. Be grateful that there are staff in school who will take this responsibility – but only if you tell them about it.

It is important to get abuse into perspective by knowing that it is comparatively rare. It is possible to go through a working life and never come across an abused child.

Links

Bullying
Discipline
Emotional development
Intellectual development
Linguistic development
Physical development
Relationships with pupils
Social development
Working with other adults

Strategies

What do you do? What is your duty of care?

- Take responsibility to teach about abuse and other issues that are about safety, e.g. bullying.
- Help children to know when to tell an adult about a concern.
- Have a classroom that is high on warmth, low on criticism.
- Develop trust between you and those you teach.
- If you suspect non-accidental physical damage or any other form of abuse, don't panic. Respond promptly and professionally – know the codes of conduct and procedures for your school – be careful to apply them. Be aware that you cannot promise the child not to tell. In incidents of abuse you may not offer confidentiality to the child. It is better to take action that later has a reasonable explanation, than to have a child suffer.
- Don't make a drama out of a crisis. Act on a 'need to know' basis. Only tell the people who are responsible for taking further action.
- As soon as you can, WRITE DOWN time, place, people, context. If matters go to court you will need a written record of the actions you took.
- If things looks as if they may go to law, don't be your own lawyer, use support services.

Further reading

Used with caution the World Wide Web is a sensible way to further research this area because it give access to up-to-date information.

The official websites are:

www.everychildmatters.gov.uk/socialcare/safeguarding/workingtogether
www.teachernet.gov.uk/wholeschool/familyandcommunity/childprotection

Both these sites have useful links. In particular, 'What to do if you're worried if a child is abused' (Crown copyright 2005, reference number 31553) is full of very important guidance and can be downloaded from Teachernet.

Most teachers' professional organisations and unions have access to expert advice on all aspects of child protection and other child safety issues. For example, www.data.teachers.org.uk gets you to the National Union of Teachers site.

TDA reference

Q21(a, b).

Code of Practice

This is a brief summary of some aspects of the Special Educational Needs Code of Practice (CoP) as it applies to schools in England.

The definition of Special Educational Needs

Children with SEN have learning difficulties that need special provision, i.e.:

a. difficulties in learning, significantly greater than the majority of children at the same age; or
b. have a disability which prevents or hinders them from making use of educational facilities of a kind generally provided for children of the same age in schools within the area of the local educational authority.

(Section 312, Education Act, 1996)

Further definitions of SEN come from the Children Act 1989 (Section 17 (11)). These include children with disabilities such as 'blind, deaf or dumb or suffers from mental disorder of any kind or is substantially and permanently handicapped by illness, injury or congenital deformity or such other disability as may be prescribed'.

Disability Discrimination Act 1995 (Section 1(1)) adds children with disabilities that have a 'substantial or long term adverse effect ... on ... day-to-day activities' to the list of definitions.

The CoP was revised in 2002 to take account of Education Act (1991) and Special Educational Needs and Disability Act (2001).

The Code of Practice sets out some principles

These are that a child with SEN should have his or her needs met, normally in mainstream schools or early years' settings.

- A child with SEN should have his/her views sought and taken into account.
- The parent's role in supporting the education of their child is recognized as vital.
- A child with SEN should have access to a broad, balanced and relevant curriculum (for both the Foundation stage, i.e. three to five years and National Curriculum, i.e. five years old and beyond).

Some of the success criteria in the CoP

The plan for each child identifies ways that all a child's needs are met, taking account cultural needs, management needs and the way resources are best used in schools; that pupils are identified early and that 'best practice' is exploited. The child's wishes and the parents' and carers' views should be taken into account. The assessment of need is within prescribed time limits. Statements about each child are clear, detailed, time limited, the monitoring is specified and annually reviewed. It is expected that, if the parents and carers and the child want him/her to be educated in a mainstream school, this will happen. At the same time, the CoP recognizes that a very small number of children have conditions so severe as to make this impractical. Some specialist provision will remain.

Under the CoP, *parents* (anyone with responsibility for the learner) are expected to be actively involved in the decisions made about their child. Account has to be taken of their views, attitudes, emotional investment and differing perspectives about the process, the child, the people involved and the range of provision. The parents' and carers' needs have to be met in setting up meetings, when these are and where they are held should be convenient for them. They must be told when a SEN is first identified for their child. They must be kept informed throughout schooling and involved in decision making. They have duties and responsibilities as well.

Pupils have to be involved in decisions made about them. Account has to be taken of their age, maturity and capability when doing this. They are to be involved in Individual Educational Plans (IEPs) made for them, and in the assessment process. As they get towards the end of schooling they are expected to start to take a lead role in what they are going to do with the rest of their lives.

In early years settings (i.e. before school at age five there is an emphasis on early identification of need. The adoption of a 'graduated approach' is expected. Early Years Action (EYA) includes this cycle:

- identifying the need
- doing what seems best to meet that need
- assessing progress
- stopping when the need is successfully met.

If it is not, EYA continues, going through the cycle again, trying different approaches. If the child is not making adequate progress under EYA, this triggers outside advice and support. This is Early Years Action Plus (EYA+) with, for under-fives, informal assessment every six months and, at age five, detailed information to parents and carers to inform transfer decisions. If the child is in school the Special Educational Needs Coordinator (SENCO, see below) takes this action. In other settings it will be someone with day-to-day contact with the child.

Schools (from age five) use information that already exists with a focus of 'can do' and 'needs to learn'. This action will use assessments and other tests to make judgements about need. During schooling, the teachers will use ongoing observations, assessment and feedback in planning to meet needs. Joint home–school learning approaches will be encouraged. Differentiation is assumed to be happening for *all* the children in school. In the School Action (SA) phase a 'graduated approach' continues in the way outlined for EYA. If the child is not making sufficient progress, then the school will move to School Action Plus (SA+). SA+ may include the writing of an Individual Education Plan (IEP) where differentiation is over and above what would normally be expected. The advice of specialists and resources from beyond the school may be used. Parents and carers and pupil involvement remains active.

The CoP has provision to include early or interim reports sent for *children at risk of serious disaffection or exclusion*. These children can be dealt with under SA and SA+.

English as an additional language is not equated with SEN although it is recognized as requiring extra resources.

Local authorites (LAs) are responsible for making sure that all schools and educational settings carry out the principles in the CoP.

Each child with SEN has an Annual Review. However, the IEP which is a working document is likely to be reviewed much more regularly. The IEP makes clear the additional or different activities that are needed to meet the learner's needs. The IEP should be under continuous review and should be reviewed twice each year. Where pupils are grouped for instruction to meet their needs a Group Educational Plan (GEP) may replace an IEP.

In Year 9 a link is made with *Connexions* for all students (a multi-agency service for young people). As with all other students, this is to help the student with SEN to make decisions about what to do at the end of school years. By Year 11 the reviews of the young person's progress will have much more involvement of agencies beyond the school.

The Special Educational Needs Coordinator (SENCO) has a significant role in all this. It is strategic, determining policy and whole-school approaches to teaching and learning for children with SEN. It requires significant time to fulfil the role. In a school with many children with barriers to learning, it may leave time for no other duties. It has status, the SENCO is a senior manager with a special role in communication with the teaching team, i.e. teachers and teaching assistants, parents and carers and pupils, and with those beyond the school. At any stage other professionals may be involved in information gathering and decision making about the learner. Inter-agency working is often coordinated through the SENCO. Part of the CoP is concerned with training and improving skills for both the SENCO and all those working with children with SEN both within and beyond the educational setting.

Some children, even after SA and SA+ still don't make much progress. For these pupils, the SENCO in consultation with colleagues, the parents and carers and the child, and often an outside agency will start the *statutory assessment* process. The LA will usually only agree to statutory assessment if it is demonstrated that everything has been tried at EYA/SA and EYA+/SA+. There will be many children in EYA/SA and EYA+/SA+, but comparatively few will require statutory assessment. This is the point at which LA decisions become important. Children whose needs are assessed will not automatically be granted a statement. The school, parents and carers and child may be asked to go back to EYA+/SA+, with perhaps more support. Statements, once written, generate additional LA support and use centrally held resources (i.e. specialist staff). There has to be a prompt and flexible response to newly identified needs. The *statement* must be a precise description of provision for the child with SEN. Some children have needs identified at a very early age. They have statements before they start formal education.

In the CoP it is expected that LAs and schools will work in partnership. They are expected to use their best endeavours to meet needs, to find cost-effective solutions, to provide information about mainstream and other appropriate educational provision for parents and carers, to enable assessment to add knowledge about the child with SEN.

Links

Connexions
Inclusion
Special educational needs

Further reading

From www.teachernet.gov.uk the download DfES, *Special Educational Needs: Toolkit* has all the details about the CoP.

TDA references

Q19, Q20.

Communicating clearly

Communicating clearly is an essential skill for the teacher. This involves what you have to say and how you say it. Talking to large groups is not a skill we use in everyday life, so it has to be learned. First, when planning to talk to the whole class or the whole school, consider carefully the points you wish to convey. If necessary, jot key words and phrases down on a lesson plan or small card. This will enable you to be succinct and talk to your audience rather than read to them.

During a lesson a teacher uses different voices rather like an actor. To gain attention your voice needs to be carrying and firm. It is best to keep the attention-gaining instruction short, loud enough to be heard by all, and to use a familiar instruction such as, 'Stop what you are doing, and look this way'. When attention is gained you can switch to a style appropriate to what you have to say. This might be an instructional style or a conversational style but it will be quieter so that the children have to listen and will not feel they can both talk to their friends and listen to you!

While the children are working, you will be moving round the room or working with a group and your voice will be much quieter. Occasionally you will scan the room and may use short commands or name children whose attention you want to attract. This indicates to the whole class that you are aware of them all, even though you are engaged directly with only a few. Sometimes you can praise a child in a loud voice which others can hear. This can make the child feel good and others want to work harder so that they can be praised too. If most 'loud' comments in the lesson are either instructional or positive, a better classroom atmosphere is created.

Finally, expression and variation in your voice is important. All of us like to listen to actors and storytellers. Teachers need to be a little bit of an actor and storyteller to motivate and convey enthusiasm for topics. Learn to use different tones to convey your expectations. After all, you cannot really get cross every time a child does something silly, but you can sound cross so that they know they have crossed the line of acceptability.

Links

Behaviour
Communication about learning
Discipline
Instruction
Purposeful working atmosphere
Whole-class teaching

Strategies

- Work out what you will say to the whole class.
- Plan using phrases rather than whole sentences, so that you can talk rather than read.
- Have a set phrase that gains attention and gives instruction so that the children have no choice but to pay attention.
- Make inputs interesting by using a variety of tones of voice.
- Keep instructions short and clear.
- Use the tone of your voice to indicate your approval or disapproval.
- Be clear with young children in what you say and how you say it.
- Use words and phrases to the whole class to establish 'presence'.
- Try and maintain a 'positive' classroom atmosphere.

Development

Teachers have different views on how to communicate with children. Wells (1996) summarizes a study on young children's meaning, making important conclusions on how teachers facilitate high quality conversation and guide children to reinvent knowledge. He contrasts these situations with a traditional transmission style of teaching where the teacher imparts the knowledge and the children are expected to listen and learn.

Communication can be more than oral comment. Cruickshank et al. (1979) surveyed students with the research question 'Clear teaching, what is it?' The results were summarized into the following eight responses:

1. Gives us a chance to think about what's being taught.
2. Explains something and then stops so we can think about it.

3. Shows us how to remember things.

4. Gives us enough time for practice.

5. Teaches at a pace appropriate to the topic and pupils.

6. Takes time when explaining.

7. Answers pupils' questions.

8. Stresses difficult points.

Further reading

Cruickshank, D., Kennedy, J., Bush, A. and Myers, B. (1979) 'Clear teaching – what is it?' *British Journal of Teacher Education*, 5: 1, 27–33.

Wells, G. (1996) 'Conversation and the reinvention of knowledge', in Pollard, A., *Readings for Reflective Teaching in the Primary School*, London: Continuum.

TDA reference

Q4.

Communication about learning

If children are to learn actively, then your feedback on how they're doing is extremely important. The relationship between you and those who you teach needs to be positive. If you are high on warmth (empathy) and low on criticism, this creates an ethos that is nurturing and will enable each child to do well. During the time you spend with your class you will learn about progress and achievement in many aspects of each child's life. You will learn what makes them happy and what makes them sad in their life outside school. Yard (playground) duty and other 'informal' responsibilities, including extra-curricular clubs and sport, are all important in getting to really know something about those whom you teach.

Links

Active learning
Communicating clearly
Culture
Differentiation
Expectations about pupils' learning
Feedback
Independent learning
Listening and responding to pupils

Motivation
Relationships with pupils
Self-assessment by pupils
Target-setting
Values and ethos

Strategies

Make accurate assessments about:
- the learning process – how does the child learn?
- progress towards learning objectives – what is the child learning?

Ask the child:
- how he/she learns
- about achievement.

Tell the child:
- how you think he/she learns
- about the progress towards learning objective he/she is making
- success in both the learning process and the learning objectives.

Set realistic targets for improving:
- the way the child learns
- achievement.

Both written and verbal comments should start with the positive, 'you've worked hard', 'you've really grasped this', before setting targets.

Make communication two-way, ask:
- how do you feel you've got on?
- how did you do that?
- what do you think you need to do to improve?

Help the child to set realistic and achievable goals for him/herself – targets have to challenge, but they also have to be realistic and achievable.

Development

The focus is on the learning and tasks that the children do. When they do less well, rather than blaming the children, the conversation should be about improving their work. When they do well, it is about telling them that the work is good. You will also comment on how they did the work. This places the emphasis on communicating about the process and products of learning. This approach is thought to increase motivation and to reduce the incidence of disaffection. The long-term aim is make children able to identify when they have done well and when they could do better, for themselves.

The reason for the strategies and the emphasis on what the child achieves is based on research about how learners think about success. Some put success down to luck, some to ability and some to effort. The three explanations have different outcomes. They should lead to a differentiated feedback to those whom you teach. For example, if success is down to ability then if I do better:

> it might be that I've been lucky; or it might be that I've worked harder.

Either way, 'doing better', I may think, is beyond my control. My teacher can help with this by helping me to think strategically. The questions, 'how did you do that?' and 'what do you think you need to do to improve?' are particularly useful for learners like this.

Further reading

Chaplian, R. (2000) 'Helping children to persevere and be well motivated', in Whitebread, D. (ed.) *The Psychology of Teaching and Learning in the Primary School*, London: Routledge, is a useful introduction to these ideas.

TDA reference

Q4.

Communication with parents and carers

Parents and carers, the people who care for the pupils in your class, have rights and responsibilities. Your respect for them is central to establishing and maintaining a working relationship.

Partnership with parents and carers in helping their children to become successful at school and beyond, can be achieved in many ways. With younger children contact is frequent, often on a daily basis, when someone brings and collects the child. As the child becomes more independent, contact needs to rely more on formal meetings. The social events that schools put on are hugely important in building relationships. The effort put into this aspect of schooling is important in building bridges and helping communication. However, it should always be remembered that the power relationships between teacher and parents and carers mean that partnership is likely to be uneven (for example, in school, it's you who holds the position of power – you're 'the teacher', but on home territory the parent or carer is the main decision maker).

Links

Code of Practice
Culture
Ethnicity
Homework and out-of-class work
Parents and carers
Special educational needs
Values and ethos

Strategies

- Build your reputation as a trustworthy and reliable authority by being positive and helpful.
- Prepare for meetings (both informal and formal) and written reports, which need:
  i   accurate information about the progress the child is making
  ii knowing about the child both in the class setting and beyond, their behaviour, talents, ambitions, difficulties.

Be:
- Approachable – in face-to-face meetings, smile and be pleasant; in written reports use a style that is accessible to your audience.
- A good listener to what is said and to what is meant – sometimes parents are less than direct about a worry they have.
- Responsive.
- Considerate and polite.
- Serious.
- Constructive.
- Both honest and tactful.
- Well presented – both in person and in what you write.

Development

The idea of partnership, of a shared interest, is a key to success in teacher/

parent or carer working relationships. Partnerships between parents and carers and teachers may be at several levels. In some schools there is a real sharing of responsibility for pupils' progress. Parents and carers will be well-informed about academic, social and other aspects of their child's progress in school. They'll be active in informing teachers about things at home that may influence learning in school. In others parents will also be well-informed but perhaps less confident, less concerned and less willing to share information with teachers. Some parents and carers are happiest to leave decisions to teachers. This does not mean that they are not concerned about their child's welfare, just that they see teachers as not requiring their input. Some parents and carers, and these are a concern, are uninvolved, and seem very hard to reach. However, most teachers have very comfortable and useful contacts with parents and carers. This is not necessarily a full partnership. One reason for this is that teachers are often wary that parental influence may become interference. This may be true for parents and carers too, who do not wish to reveal their home circumstances to teachers.

Further reading

Cowley, S. (2003) *How to Survive your First Year in Teaching*, London: Continuum. Chapter 10, 'Parents', deals with how to manage this aspect of your work.

Hughes, P. (2002) *Principles of Primary Education – Study Guide*, London: David Fulton. Chapter 10, 'Home-School-Community Connections', has useful suggestions on parental help in and out of school.

Thody, A., Gray, B. and Bowden, D. (2004) *The Teacher's Survival Guide*, London: Continuum. Chapter 7, 'Significant Others', is another guide how to do this.

TDA reference

Q4.

Competition

Competition is part of our society and education system (exams, grades, sports). Competition need not exclude intrinsic reward but you need to be clear about its place in the culture of your classroom.

'Competition is good for you' and 'The world is a competitive place', are two frequently heard slogans. As with all enduring slogans there is probably some truth in them. If you are able to compete, competition can be enjoyable. If you have a chance of winning, it is a highly motivating activity. It does not take long for children to work out what their individual or team chances are. Then, either they will continue to compete because they conform to what is expected of them, or they become completely de-motivated and cease to take part. If they do not join in this can be infuriating for other team members and sometimes peer pressure is successfully brought to bear.

Links

Active learning
Bullying
Discipline
Independent learning
Motivation
Rewards
Standardized tests
Summative assessment

Strategies

- Is it appropriate to make this activity competitive?
- Can all the children participating see that they can have some form of success?
- Is the reward suitable?
- Are the rules clear to all participants?
- How are you developing intrinsic motivation?

Development

Every teacher wants the children in their class to be well motivated and most teachers spend time looking for something that will motivate even the most reluctant learner. Competition is a powerful motivator but it does not work for everyone. One can consider competing against others or oneself. The choice to participate, or not, lies with the pupil, whatever pressure is brought to bear, be it punishment or reward. For the teacher it is a delicate mix between preparing children for an education system, which predominantly measures success by examination achievements, and developing a desire within children to do tasks because they are innately interesting or beneficial.

Muijs and Reynolds (2001) describe work carried out by Borich (1996) in which he describes three types of classroom, the competitive, the cooperative and the individualistic. In the competitive classroom the standards are set by the teacher, pupils give right or wrong responses, as judged by the teacher, and pupils have a sense of success or failure set against the achievement or non-achievement of these targets. In contrast the individualistic classroom encourages more independent decision making, targets are set by the students themselves and the teacher operates more in a guidance mode. Incidentally, in general, boys prefer the competitive classroom.

Further reading

Muijs, D. and Reynolds, D. (2001) *Effective Teaching: Evidence and Practice*, London: Paul Chapman.

Connexions

In English secondary education this is a new inter-agency approach which will have an impact on the inclusion agenda. Connexions is a single point of access for *all* 13 to 19 year olds to help to prepare for the transition to work and adult life.

Links

Code of Practice
Inclusion
Special educational needs

Further reading

Visit www.connexions-direct.com for further information.

TDA reference

Q18.

Creativity

Creativity is an idea that has recently re-emerged in education. First mooted in the 1960s, the idea is that education should allow pupils to be creative in their work. This is possibly a counterbalance to the fairly rigorous regimes of the Literacy and Numeracy Strategies and their dominance of primary school curriculum time in the last decade. 'Excellence and Enjoyment' (DfES, 2003) is a document produced by the British government which brings together these two major initiatives and the need for a varied and exciting curriculum. This is now referred to as 'The Primary National Strategy'.

> This document set out the vision for the future of primary education built on what has already been achieved. The vision is for a sector where high standards are obtained through a rich, varied and exciting curriculum which develops children in a range of ways.
>
> ('Excellence and Enjoyment' website)

The document frequently refers to 'creativity' but you might ask if this is the right label to use as it appears to consider creativity only in the context of art subjects and expects children to be creative within a very structured regime. It is worth considering carefully whether one can teach creativity or create an environment and teach skills which will allow children to be creative.

Links

Foundation stage
Primary National Strategy
Purposeful working atmosphere

Further reading

'The Primary National Strategy': www.standards.dfes.gov.uk/primary

'Excellence and Enjoyment' can be located on the Standards site at www.standards.dfes.gov.uk/primary/ publications/literacy/63553

Ways of introducing creativity into the classroom www.ncaction.org.uk/creativity

TDA references

Q10, Q19.

Culture

Culture is determined by the set(s) of values and experiences and traditions that individuals and groups hold. Cultural groups may be determined, for example, by language, forms of dress, ethical and religious beliefs, diet and customs. As a teacher you will have a set of expectations about the children you teach. Some of these will result from your own cultural heritage and the traditions you and your family and community have. Your awareness about other cultural groups will inform your teaching. Knowing about different cultures means that you can choose methods, resources and examples that will help your learners. It also helps to avoid misunderstandings. For example, you may think that a child who has misbehaved is being defiant because as you tell him/her off there in no eye contact. In some cultures children know that it is rude to look an adult in the eye, especially when you've displeased them. The child you think defiant may be using home rules to avert your displeasure.

Links

Communication with parents and carers
English as an additional language
Equal opportunities
Ethnicity
Relationships with pupils
Resources
Social development
Values and ethos

Strategies

Find out about the culture of those who you teach:
- ask the children
- talk to parents
- use the expertise of school staff
- find out about the community the school serves.

Respect cultural difference, take care:
- over the language you use
- to choose teaching methods and resources that are appropriate for the cultural mix in your class
- that your stereotypes, useful as they are, may need to be re-examined from time to time
- to celebrate cultural richness (but to avoid tokenism).

Development

This entry has over-simplified a complex concept. Culture is not a fixed entity. A great many things influence individuals. Their cultural group is only one factor. A social justice agenda would place much more emphasis on the nuances of difference and equality. There is political debate around citizenship and what this is. Understanding culture, with associated ideas about tolerance, politics, conflict resolution and moral reasoning, will help to inform your opinion about this. The emotional capital invested in national identity is complex. Ethnicity is part of this. In England, though most people are white, there are Asian, black and other minority ethnic groups in the population. Each of these sub groups has a cultural identity. In some cultures the role that men and women take are clearly determined. In native English homes, as in other cultures, parenting may be varied. In many homes women may take lead the role, but this is not a universal truth. The concept of culture cannot be considered without thinking about gender, wealth and status. The entry on *Equal opportunities* offers further guidance.

Cultural differences can conflict and confuse teachers who have one set of expectations that are challenged by children who come from different backgrounds. Most people have ideas about their own identity. English nationals who are teachers, on the whole, are middle class, white and, in primary schools, female; because of this, middle-class culture may be predominant in the schools where they teach. The community culture may be quite different. Where the community culture is different to their own background, teachers may have lower expectations about academic achievement. The children you teach and their parents have ideas about how you will behave and what to expect from you. These ideas can be brought into school and may be challenging to deal with.

Further reading

See the Equal opportunities reading list.

On the web the British Council site is a helpful starting place for finding out about culture in other countries
www.britcoun.org

Johnson, E. (ed.) (2003) *ITV Cultural Diversity Guide*, London: Granada.

TDA reference

Q18.

Demonstration by the teacher

Demonstrating and explaining are both highly skilled forms of teaching. Having established your learning outcome, what it is the children are going to learn, you'll need to break down the demonstration into carefully considered steps. It helps to rehearse before working in front of the class.

Showing your class how to do something can be a highly effective teaching approach. Some procedures and skills are most effectively taught this way. Examples include showing children how to set out written work (margins, date, where to put their name, what to do about corrections, etc.) and safe ways of carrying equipment. You need to teach children precisely how you want these things done. Then they need opportunity to practise the procedure or skill. You need to check that things are as they should be. You'll probably need to remind and correct them fairly frequently to start with. Eventually procedures and skills become automatic. However, remember that a procedure or skill learned in one environment, or under one condition, will not necessarily transfer to new situations. For instance, safety rules learned in science will need to be demonstrated and taught again in craft lessons. This is concrete and holistic teaching. Children see what it is you do and then they can replicate it.

Demonstration through telling and using examples to model thinking is another highly effective teaching approach. For example, in mathematics a teacher might get at a general statement through careful questions and appropriate examples discussed in depth. Or, in English and social science subjects, to create informed opinion, the teacher may argue aloud, putting forward various points of view and the reasons why some are more convincing than others. Examples need to be carefully considered. Case studies worked through in pairs and groups, with children explaining the work and their thinking about it to each other and to the teacher, can be very useful. The work often needs to be placed in a sequence of practice, review and then application to new situations.

Links

Active learning
Communicating clearly
Communication about learning
Independent learning
Instruction
Learning styles
Pace
Safety
Skills and strategies
Whole-class teaching

Strategies

Before you start:

- Make sure that you have everything you need for the demonstration.
- Make sure you are absolutely accurate in the demonstration.
- Think carefully about pace; be slow enough to be clear, but not so slow that it's boring.
- Make sure you've thought about safety.
- Practise your demonstration – rehearse your questions, predict possible answers, think about what might go wrong and what you'll do to put things right.

In class:

- Move children so that everyone can clearly see what it is you are demonstrating.
- Tell them exactly what it is that is being demonstrated.
- 'Think aloud', modelling the procedure, skill and thinking.
- Use carefully chosen questions.
- Listen and respond to answers.
- When appropriate get children to predict what might happen.
- Have some poor examples for children to critique.
- Do some examples steps by step.
- If you are demonstrating a way of thinking, make the 'laws' of the subject explicit.
- If you are demonstrating a way of thinking, use case studies to show how ideas are used in practice.
- Give opportunities to practise with your support.
- Teach children how to check for themselves.
- Be prepared to re-teach until everyone has understood and can do what is required.

Development

Much of your teaching will be demonstration so it's worth thinking about what makes it effective for the learner. Sousa (2001) reminds us that the brain responds positively to humour, movement, using all the senses; touch, smell, feel as well as listening. Humour, for example, has physiological benefits in that it wakes the brain up and, used with care, it is an attention grabber. It helps to create a positive environment for learning and it helps people to remember.

Further reading

Muijs, D. and Reynolds, D. (2005) *Effective Teaching: Evidence and Practice* (2nd Ed.), London: Sage. Chapter 2, 'Direct Instruction', is a useful starting place.

Sousa, D. A. (2001) *How the Brain Learns*, Thousand Oaks: Corwin.

TDA reference

Q25(a).

Differentiation

All groups of pupils have a range of ability and needs. As a student teacher or new teacher to the school, collecting information about pupils' needs and abilities begins on preliminary visits. Through observation, questioning and listening to pupils, talking to the teacher and looking at records you should be able to acquire sufficient information to plan detailed schemes. At first you will plan work which you think is appropriate for a particular group of pupils, but as you get to know them and you observe their responses you will be able to plan the next piece of work so that it more closely matches what they need. This will probably involve modifying your medium-term planning as you go along. Remember, your planning needs to include consideration of gender, culture and race as well as academic performance.

You can differentiate your teaching in three ways:

1. by task
2. by outcome
3. by support.

Some tasks can be given to all the pupils and they will be able to respond and learn from them. The task allows them to respond at their own level, this is called differentiation by outcome. Other tasks will only benefit certain groups, therefore different tasks or variations of the original task are given to each group. This is called differentiation by task.

When you differentiate by support you will be responding to individual needs. This could involve helping individuals, but also adapting goals as you work with the children. For example, when you see an able child has clearly understood the work set, you might reduce the practice task and set him/her a more challenging task where he/she has to apply the information. If another child is struggling you might simplify the task or give a task which underpins the one he/she is attempting.

By differentiating tasks you are trying to facilitate learning. By matching the task to the children's ability you are enabling them to build on prior knowledge and move forward. If the task is well matched the child will engage in the task and learn from doing it.

Links

Able children
Active learning
Group work
Independent learning
Questioning
Whole-class teaching

Strategies

- Collect information about level of performance and past experience prior to medium-term planning.
- Select grouping appropriate to the learning objective. (If all the pupils cannot respond, differentiation needs to occur.)
- Make minor adjustments to objectives, if necessary, as you work with the children. (This involves having thought about possible extensions and simplifications when planning the lesson.)

Development

While everyone recognizes that children learn at different paces and there is a range of ability in every age group, there is little agreement on how best to cater for the range. This is probably because there is no solution which is entirely obvious. Some primary schools run mixed ability classes throughout the timetable, some schools set for certain subjects such as mathematics and some schools set the children for the whole timetable (sometimes called streaming). Even within mixed ability classes some grouping will probably take place, either all the time or partially with different groups for different subjects. While there is a trend to whole class teaching, personalized learning is also being thought about. This means that students' differentiation needs are catered for in a different ways. In class various levels and expectations of different students will occur. Beyond classwork, the curriculum will need to be further differentiated to meet the needs of individuals and groups.

There is evidence that placing children in ability groups has an effect on learning and self-esteem. Brophy and Good (1970) found that there was a sequence of low self-esteem, low teacher expectation generated by grouping students in ability groups which contributed to low performance. Boaler et al. (2000) have explored students' perceptions at secondary school level and raised some thoughtful issues well worth considering. Setting in primary schools in mathematics in the United Kingdom has increased since the 1980s, ostensibly to meet the demands of the new curriculum. This research was carried out with 13 and 14 year olds moving from mixed ability to sets in mathematics. They found little evidence that students felt they were in a better learning environment. The results indicated that the lower sets generated low student self-esteem and low expectation from teachers. This was poorly justified by a very small percentage of able children who coped with the speed of work in the top set. Teachers tended not to differentiate within lessons and a whole-class teaching model dominated in set situations. Many children appeared to find the single pace difficult to respond to.

Further reading

Boaler, J., Wiliam, D. and Brown, M. (2000) 'Students' experience of ability grouping – disaffection, polarisation and the construction of failure', *British Educational Research Journal*, 26: 5, 631–48.

Brophy, J. and Good, T. (1970) 'Teachers' communication of differential expectations for children's classroom performance: some behavioural data', *Journal of Educational Psychology*, 61, 365–74.

TDA reference

Q19.

Discipline

Discipline helps children behave acceptably in school. Discipline is intended to repress and redirect misbehaviour. Over time, the goal is to reduce the need for teacher intervention so that children learn to control themselves. Discipline is about the ways that children behave towards each other and to their teachers and the ways that teachers and the other adults in school, behave towards children. The rules that will be implemented must take account of the needs of the whole child, the needs of society as a whole and for good order in the school.

The school behaviour policy establishes what it is that teachers and teaching assistants do about discipline. The values held by school staff and implemented in the behaviour policy may conflict with those held by the parents and carers. This means that children may find that behaviour accepted at home has to be modified for school. Establishing a common set of values is never going to be easy. Teaching teams may not agree with each other about what is acceptable behaviour. Time and effort has to be made to work through to an agreed set of values to underpin the school behaviour policy. Schools that tackle this through involving the children, parents and carers, and the community often develop very successful policies. School becomes the place where the child is made aware of and learns to deal with the similarities and differences between the values that occur at home, at school, in the street and, eventually, at work.

Links

Bullying
Culture
Emotional development
Equal opportunities
Ethnicity
Inclusion
Relationships with pupils
Safety
Values and ethos
Working with parents and carers, professionals and adults

Strategies

I will implement school rules fairly by:

- Having high expectations:
  i setting high standards of behaviour e.g. treating children politely by using their names and a pleasant but firm tone of voice.
  ii through carefully teaching the rules e.g. that 'sit down, thank-you' means put your bottom on your chair and your two feet and the four chair legs on the floor, that turn taking means listening and responding – not everyone talking at once.
- Being aware of the needs of the children and taking account of their age and experience:
  i by knowing that not all children find conforming to the rules easy, by knowing who these children are and increasing the behaviour demands in small steps and rewarding even the smallest improvement.
  ii by being aware that school rules and the way I interpret them may severely conflict with the home rules or lack of rule, realizing that the match between the child's expectations and mine may need to be negotiated, allowing time for the child to come to terms and deal with this conflict.
- Developing children's understanding of the need for safety and security and risk in their own development, thus increasing their ability to be independent learners and moving them towards autonomy by, for example, offering choice; in activities, in making decisions about classroom routines and in selecting appropriate rewards and punishments.

- Knowing about cultural, racial differences and expectations, treating these differences respectfully and using this knowledge to reward and punish appropriately.
- Developing the child's moral and social understanding:
  i recognizing that the classroom is one place where social understanding can be developed by raising and dealing with, for example, moral dilemmas such as 'when is it right to tell?' through discussion and group work.

Development

Misbehaviour is behaviour considered to be inappropriate in the context in which it occurs. In school this will include:

- aggression – both physical and verbal and including bullying.
- immorality – lying, cheating, stealing.
- defiance.
- class disruption – where children talk out of turn or hinder each other.
- being off task – day dreaming, text messaging, the American expression is *goofing off.*

The last two, while minor in themselves, constitute the most frequent inter-ruptions to teaching and learning. Many school behaviour policies put considerable emphasis on reducing disruptions and off-task behaviour through carefully managing the teaching and learning in classrooms. The first three may be addressed in a number of ways. For example, reducing opportunities for bullying by having 'befrienders', children trained to look after those who find the playground difficult. Teachers use techniques such as 'circle time' to work on developing a strong class ethos in which pupils are empowered to, for example:

- deal with issues of right and wrong.
- decide what is and is not acceptable behaviour.
- discuss what working well means.
- explore how to resist peer pressure.
- address current moral issues.

Punishment for failing to keep to rules also has to be considered. Punishment has to be just and must not deny the child access to the curriculum. The really serious 'telling off', by you or a more senior teacher can be effective. The telling off has a number of steps, these may include:

- Identification of the misdemeanour (what the child did, e.g., 'The rule in our school is that we treat each other well, in the playground, you hit John, that breaks our rule').

- The consequences of the child's action in breaking the rules ('John was hit and that hurt him, he has a bruise').
- Getting the child to acknowledge that the rule was broken ('Did you know that Mrs Smith saw you hit John?' Use other sources of evidence if you meet resistance).
- A set of actions for preventing repetition agreed with the child.

The loss of privilege can be effective. The point is to keep focused on what the child did, 'you are being punishing for breaking our rule', not because 'you're bad'.

To be successful, the child must regard the punishment awarded as fair. A way must be offered to enable the child to learn to avoid repeating the offence.

Further reading

Cowley, S. (2003) *Getting the Buggers to Behave* (2nd edn), London: Continuum.

Porter, L. (2000) *Behaviour in Schools: Theory and Practice for Teachers*, Buckingham: Open University.

Rodgers, B. (2000, UK edition) *Behaviour Management: A Whole School Approach*, London: Paul Chapman.

Rodgers, B. (2004) *Behaviour Recovery* (2nd edn), London: Paul Chapman.

TDA references

Q10, Q30, Q31.

Displays

Displays can be informative, rewarding or interactive. A teacher may decide to put up a display as a stimulus for a new topic. This raises the children's awareness of what is to come and gives them time to seek out contributions. Children, like adults, like to know the programme ahead of the event, especially if they are required to contribute. Children like to see their own work on display. This is rewarding and motivating for them. The purpose of interactive displays is to allow learning to take place through children taking some action prompted by the display. The children visit the site and manipulate the materials physically or mentally. This offers an opportunity for reinforcement of something that has taken place in a lesson, or an opportunity to extend learning on a topic, therefore this type of display is particularly useful at either end of the ability range. Examples of such a display might be sorting shapes, interpreting graphs, making circuits, setting the table, interpreting maps, the role-play corner or a computer program. The advantages of the interactive display are that the teacher can be elsewhere in the classroom.

All displays should be well presented. If there is sufficient paper, double mounting helps to show work at its best. Neat titles and labelling with vertical and horizontal alignment give a professional look. Sometimes a few items look better than a crowded board. Changes in texture and pattern on the background add variety and depth to the overall look.

Link

Purposeful working atmosphere

Strategies

- Use a variety of types of display, interactive, stimulus, quality completed work.
- In medium-term planning identify lessons which will generate display materials.
- In medium-term planning decide which topics could be supported by an interactive display.
- In medium-term planning identify the resources you need to acquire, in time for you to find them.
- If a lesson is going to provide display material plan an appropriate pupil output.
- Over several weeks, ensure each child has a piece of quality work displayed.
- Double mount work where appropriate.
- Plan the layout of the display, use pins to arrange it before stapling, gluing or blu-tacking.
- Label clearly so that visitors to your room understand what the display is about.

TDA reference

Q25(a).

Emotional development

Being able to make judgements about another's feelings, the emotional state, develops from birth. Judgements about emotion are made about the continuum of happiness to sadness; the emotions of fear, anger, rage, guilt and shame. Through childhood into early adolescence an ability to understand how others feel becomes increasingly sophisticated. As the child's intellectual understanding develops, it seems that more than one emotion and the relationship between them becomes established, e.g. by eight years old many children will say things like, 'I'm cross when I'm interrupted, but I'm happy to go out to play'.

Babies connect first with those who care for them. Adults are able to reinforce the expressions that their six to eight-week-old babies make. Smiles are met with smiles; facial expressions are used to monitor the supposed emotion. This seems to be the beginning of developing a range of emotions. The baby's smiles are gradually given more readily to the adults who make most difference to him/her. Seven to nine-month-old babies show 'stranger distress' (Sroufe, 1996); the emotions of fear and anger also develop at about this time. Much of the display of emotion seems to be part of intellectual growth. There seems no doubt that toddlers learn, from the reactions of others, a whole range of emotions and how to show these. For example, by age two, infants will switch from pouting to crying if this is to their advantage.

Children move, over time, from having others help them control their emotions, to being more able to do this for themselves. Some researchers suggest that emotional regulation goes on throughout our life span (Thompson, 1991). Individuals vary hugely in the amount of self-regulation displayed. Think how easily some people cry, while others seem unable to show any emotions.

There are two areas of study that are associated with our understanding of emotion. One is temperament. You'll know the sort of person that you are, for example, you might 'be able to argue for England', or you might be easy going, taking everything in your stride. Your temperament is closely tied to your emotional type. The other area of study is the work on attachment between babies and parents and carers. Early nurturing and differences in child care may make a difference to emotional development. These two aspects begin to explain why children may react differently in the classroom.

Links

Intellectual development
Linguistic development
Social development

Further reading

Smith, P. K., Cowie, H. and Blades, M. (2003) *Understanding Children's Development*, (4th edn), Oxford: Blackwell. Chapter 6 explores these ideas in more detail.

Sroufe, L. A. (1996) *Emotional Development: The Organization of Emotional Life in the Early Years*, New York: Wiley.

Thompson, R. A. (1991) 'Emotional Regulation and Emotional Development', *Educational Psychology Review*, 3, 269–307.

TDA reference

Q18.

English as an additional language

English as an additional language (EAL) is an everyday experience in many classrooms. In England 'over half a million children do not have English as a first language' (DfEE, 1997: 34) Every teacher is expected to promote EAL in their teaching. The question is, does spoken and written language and reading develop 'naturally' or does something have to be done about it in school? Often the natural approach works quite well, especially for very young children who may seem to learn easily and rapidly. After they are about eight years old some bilingual children seem not to progress as well as others. It appears that there may be a barrier to achieving in school if we leave the teaching of English to chance. Many schools have a specific policy, curriculum and staff with expertise for success in EAL which you will need to use.

Links

Culture
Equal opportunities
Ethnicity
Linguistic development

Strategies

First, establish some facts:

- What country and language(s)?
- Refugee or migrant? (Think of culture shock for both, think of additional stresses of being a refugee.)
- How much English is spoken at home?
- Are there other children or adults in school with the same language?

Then do what you can to promote and maintain the child's first language:

- Find someone who speaks the child's language.
- Continue the learning in the child's own language as much and for as long as possible.
- Remember listening (getting the child to hear English) precedes talking and speech precedes reading and writing.
- It is also worth reminding yourself that the conventions of English, where we read from left to right and the writing 'sits' on the line, may be very different to the child's own language.

Development

Many children who are learning EAL grow up to be fluent and literate in English. They may also speak their first language well but not always read or write it. If we insist that children only speak English we are making a statement about the value we place on homes and families. The child's heritage needs to be valued. The language of the home and the community need to be celebrated. Ideally, we might want to promote bilingualism or even multilingualism. This means that while we expect children to use English for communication both in spoken and written form, and to know about its rules, grammar and conventions; we would at the same time, be actively promoting the child's first and additional languages. This is a cross-curricular, cross-phase challenge. Children with EAL offer a remarkable enrichment to the life of a school.

Further reading

DfEE (1997) *Excellence in Schools*, London: Stationery Office.

Mohan, B., Leung, C. and Davidson, C. (eds) (2001) *English as a Second Language in the Mainstream: Teaching, Learning and Identity*, London: Longman.

TDA references

Q18, Q19.

Equal opportunities

A useful place to start is to think about who we are and what contributes to our values. This list is not comprehensive, but think about:

- your *gender* including sexual orientation
- what you look like, your *physical appearance*, things like race, disability, age
- the sort of *family* you come from, nuclear, extended, single parent . . .
- your *religion and culture*
- your ability to *communicate*, including your *language*, standard English dialect, Yorkshire dialect, English as an additional language . . .
- *where you live*, inner city, suburbs, in the country. . .
- and, perhaps most importantly, your *wealth* or *status*, i.e. middle income, low income, professional job, clerical job, unskilled job.

Some of these, maybe all of them, will contribute to your identity. *Every Child Matters* (Children Act, 2004) has equality as a priority. This means recognizing that teaching is not a neutral activity, so your values and who you are, will have an effect on those who you teach. Equal opportunities is about being inclusive in the way you deal with all pupils. Treating all children the same will not serve. To be fair you have to meet the needs of individuals as far as you can. Children's attitudes to school come from their home and their community. Often these might conflict with teachers' norms. Your expectations and theirs may not match. Their experience of things like the way you talk might be unfamiliar. When you ask once, at home they may be nagged. What you say as a joke may be misunderstood, regarded as offensive or even as racist. In your teaching, help all children to:

- value themselves
- find similarities between their own lives and the lives of others
- learn from each other
- not feel that they are better than others because of their race, gender or wealth.

Links

Culture
English as an additional language
Ethnicity
Expectations about pupils' learning
Gender
Inclusion
Resources
Rewards

Strategies

Create an inclusive classroom in which:

- You are conscious that your own attitudes are influential by, for example:
  i   making a real effort to get unfamiliar names correct
  ii valuing the process of learning as well as the product
  iii avoiding remarks that start, 'girls don't . . .', 'boys don't . . .'
  iv setting high expectations about success.
- Children's home experience is valued by, for example, building a partnership with parents and carers which enables you to emphasize the similarities and positive aspects of different families' life at home.
- You deal with questions about gender, race and disability frankly and honestly, for example:
  i   getting children to describe how they look using facts, eye colour, skin colour, body parts.

- You deal with any name calling sensitively:
  i support the victim
  ii encourage other ways of dealing with feelings through, for example, circle time
  iii reference to school policy.
- Adult to adult relationships in school provide positive role models for children, for example, by distribution of roles that avoids gender bias.
- Your teaching is planned and delivered with equality of opportunity always considered. Plan to:
  i use children's prior experience
  ii use collaborative group work
  iii ensure that girls, minority ethnic children and boys all get to take leading roles
  iv differentiate tasks
  v allow for same-sex paired work
  vi allow for first language to be used in pair work
  vii choose resources that are checked for bias, use positive images are up-to-date.
- In predominantly white schools ensure that the curriculum reflects multi-racial society.

Development

This is a complex area and one where it is easy to feel 'in the wrong'. At a personal level it often seems too hard to be fair to all the children in the class all the time. Some children do need more of your attention and time at particular points. If you feel this is happening too often, you should do something about it. One way is to consciously limit yourself to spending slightly less time with more demanding children and slightly more time with those who less often get your full attention.

Further reading

Cole, M., Hill, D. and Shan, S. (eds) (1997) *Promoting Equality in Primary Schools*, London: Cassell. One of the most comprehensive textbooks around this deals both with the theoretical background and the practical outcomes for teachers.

Sheila, A. (2002) 'Dialogues with difference: teaching equality in primary classrooms,' in Moyle, J. and Robinson, G. (eds) *Beginning Teaching: Beginning Learning in Primary Education* (2nd edn), Buckingham: Open University.

There are very good sources on the web:

www.cre.gov.uk has good links to many educational resources

www.teachernet. gov.uk

www.everychildmatters.gov.uk/publication *Every Child Matters: Change for Children* is a useful link.

TDA references

Q18, Q19.

Ethnicity

In the last full census UK population of approximately 54 million about six per cent are from minority ethnic groups (1991 census figures). Ballard and Kalra (1994: 11) estimate that about 11 per cent of the school population are from minority ethnic groups. The drive from the UK government is to ensure that all children in our schools achieve high standards. In the past there is evidence that some groups, for example, both Afro-Caribbean pupils (Gillborn and Mirza, 2000) and white boys from working-class backgrounds are doing less well in public examinations and national tests. For teachers in England, developing an understanding and having a positive attitude about children from different ethnic backgrounds, along with a commitment to their success is a requirement (Children Act 1989, 2004) as well as a professional standard. As a teacher you will have a set of expectations about the children you teach. In part this will result from your own ethnicity. Your race, like your status in society and your gender, raises expectations in the children you teach and from their parents and carers. They will come to school with attitudes informed by their families' experience in the community. Home behaviour towards adults may be very different from your own. Your awareness about other ethnic groups will inform your teaching. Knowing about differences means that you can choose methods, resources and examples that will help your learners. It also helps to avoid misunderstandings and false expectations.

Links

Culture
Equal opportunities
Gender

Strategies

See strategies suggested for *Equal opportunities.*

Development

Cole (1997: 53) argues that in UK schools there are three approaches to education and that each is a strongly held position. Some schools have a monocultural attitude that 'attempts to make everyone "socially and culturally British"'. Others adopt a multicultural policy that celebrates cultural and religious difference. The last group adopts anti-racist policies that actively challenge all aspects of discrimination. Any of the above positions seem to place schooling as central in attitude forming. This would suggest that what teachers do about this issue is important.

Further reading

Ballard, R. and Kalra, V. S. (1994) *Ethnic Dimensions of the 1991 Census: A Preliminary Report*, Manchester: University of Manchester Census Group.

Cole, M. (1997) 'Equality and primary education: what are the conceptual issues?', in Cole, M., Hill, D. and Shan, S. (eds) *Promoting Equality in Primary Schools*, London: Cassell.

Gillborn, D. and Mirza, H. S. (2000) *Educational Inequality: Mapping Race, Class and Gender. A Synthesis of Research Evidence*, London: Ofsted (website www.ofsted.gov.uk)

www.everychildmatters.gov.uk/publication *Every Child matters: Change for children* is a useful link.

TDA reference

Q19.

Evaluating lessons (assessing the meeting of learning objectives)

Lessons are evaluated for several reasons. The main one is to ensure learning has taken place. You will need to assess whether the children have met the set objective(s). If they have, this will inform you that the lesson was effective and will provide information for individual records. When learning has not taken place it is important to reflect on what has happened and make decisions about adjusting the approach. It might be that the objective was not appropriate for all or some of the children. Maybe it was too hard or too easy, and because of this the children did not engage in the work. It might be that the planned activities did not match and support the objective. Possibly they learned something else or were confused. Maybe your teaching techniques still need to be developed so that a purposeful working atmosphere can be created. Maybe a combination of snowfall, dentist and school photographer has completely disrupted the lesson. In this case, even the best teachers give in gracefully.

Once you have analysed the lesson you need to make decisions about how you will approach the next lesson. Your decided action might be appropriate for all your lessons or a strategy you plan to use during the teaching of that particular subject or group.

Links

Active learning
Formative assessment
Independent learning
Learning objectives
Medium-term planning
Summative assessment
Target-setting

Strategies

A simple evaluation of the lesson might fall into the following categories:

Children	Noted individual performance to records/who needs help.
Activity	Did the activities support the objectives well and would I use them again?
Teacher	What teacher skills did I use well/need to change?

Development

There are a lot of things which can go wrong with lessons. Even for the best teachers, lessons which go really well are not as common as people think. One aim is to ensure that all lessons are of a reasonable quality. With good preparation and a continuing proactive approach to improving your teaching skills this should come about.

Moyles (1995: 109–10) describes the reflective process of evaluating lessons and medium-term plans:

What we are essentially assessing is to what extent the children (and you) have been able to:
- reach the objectives set for them in planning;
- develop appropriate attitudes and opinions;
- reach high standards and offer quality outcomes;
- deal with the rates at which they learn;
- find out about their strengths and weaknesses;
- understand what learning should take place next for children to progress;
- know what activities or experiences should now be provided or repeated and what differentiated experiences are needed for which children.

Further reading

Moyles, J. (ed.) (1995) *Beginning Teaching: Beginning Learning in Primary Education*, Buckingham: Open University Press.

TDA reference

Q29.

Expectations about pupils' learning (Challenge)

Challenge is about engaging children in thinking and working on the borders of their knowledge. Educational experience is a mixture of challenge, routine and review. Challenging children gives them the opportunity to take risks, to apply knowledge, to adopt new understanding, to work in context and to experience the thrill of being discoverers. This last is a highly motivating and engaging feeling.

Consider that most of the adult world is about routine and challenge. We do need to educate children to sustain routine, meet challenge and deal with both. Also, remember that all children can be challenged at their own level. It is not just a target for able pupils.

Children like to know where they are so that they have some control over the day. They also enjoy revisiting because it reaffirms their belief that there are things they can do and be successful at. Games, stories and computer programs are good examples of revisiting situations. They also like challenge where they are required to draw on their knowledge to resolve unfamiliar situations.

Teachers like to present a range of situations too. There are the times when routine is strong and skills and knowledge are built in a formal way without having to set up new procedures, for example, spellings, skill-building exercises, diary writing. Then there are times when the teacher wants children to use the knowledge and skills they have acquired. This could be by asking children to bring their problem-solving skills to new situations which will lead to new learning or a chance to apply knowledge to a problem in a context they have already worked on.

Links

Able children
Active learning
Differentiation
Foundation Stage
Independent learning
Motivation

Primary National Strategy
Problem solving
Thinking skills

Strategies

- Provide a balance through the week of the type of work provided; routine, new learning, review/ consolidation, challenge.
- Ensure children have the opportunity to apply their knowledge in new contexts.
- Differentiate work where possible.
- Have lots of problem solving!

Development

There is a considerable body of evidence building, from the time of Piaget through to present day research into thinking skills, that problem solving contributes to developing effective learning skills. Challenging a person's thinking is what forces them to adjust or confirm the views they already hold. Discussing how to solve problems means a person has to articulate their ideas and have others comment on them. This is a strong strategy for clarifying and remembering. Maybe this is the territory where learning, which may be transferred to other new situations, takes place.

On a more individual note, it is worth reflecting on what our expectations are of particular children. Is it wise to form the view that they cannot possibly solve problems, that they are only capable of copying, that they can only manage book 4, that they need to work in this maths group because they are of low ability in language skills? Our perceptions of children are clearly conveyed by our communications with them. If we have low expectations, children will believe that is all they are capable of. We need to be very careful about what we convey and expect.

TDA references

Q1, Q18, Q19.

Explaining

Teaching by explanation is an effective way of encouraging learning. Poor explanation will be a source of frustration and tension in class. Careful preparation is a key to engaging pupils. Getting the mixture of instruction, questioning and the pace of your whole-class teaching is important. If children have not understood, you need to act. You could go over the explanation with the whole class or with groups or with individuals. If this happens often, you will need to alter the way you explain. Children who need you to go over what you have just explained to the whole class, just for them, can be time consuming. Think about the additional explanation that these pupils will need and how you can plan this into the session. You may be able to use teaching assistants to do this, or you may need to set the class going on activities and return afterwards to these pupils.

Links

Communicating clearly
Instruction
Pace
Questioning
Working with parents and carers, professionals and other adults

Strategies

- Make sure that you understand what you are explaining.
- Teach new material as soon as you have pupils' attention in a lesson.
- Make good use of any additional adults to support children who are unclear about what they are to do or are slow starting tasks.
- Take account of pupils' previous knowledge and experience of the topic.
- Link your explanation to pupils' knowledge, experience and interests.
- Use language that your pupils can understand.
- Tell pupils what it is that they are going to learn.
- Break your explanation into small steps.
- Use carefully chosen examples, have several different examples.
- Allow time for practice and rehearsal.
- Review your explanation with pupils at the end the lesson.

Development

Sousa's (2001) analysis of a 40-minute lesson suggests that the first 20 minutes is the best time to introduce new information. He suggests that you should avoid asking pupils about the topic in the introduction to your explanation. This is because if you get a wrong answer at this point from pupils, it will 'contaminate' the explanation. The next 10 to 15 minutes should be used to allow pupils to engage on activities related to the new topic. The last chunk of time gives you a chance to review the new knowledge the pupils have. This is one style of teaching. Another school of thought would recommend a less formal approach where explanations follows challenge.

Further reading

Sousa, D. A. (2001) *How the Brain Learns* (2nd edn), Thousand Oaks: Corwin.

Wragg, E. C. and Brown, G. (2001) *Explaining in the Primary School* (2nd edn), London: RoutledgeFalmer. A very useful self-help text.

TDA reference

Q25(c).

Feedback

Feedback is the provision of an evaluation on a piece of work or action. The feedback can be formal or informal and can come from a variety of sources. The usual person to provide feedback is the teacher, but there are occasions when appreciation is shown by others, such as the headteacher, parents at assemblies and other adults in the classroom.

As the teacher you will provide informal feedback as you respond in whole-class, group and individual situations. Encouraging pupils' explanations about a task and the work they have done will help them to articulate their views. If you can then encourage pupils to suggest what action needs to be taken you are beginning to establish an approach to pupils' self-evaluation. Effective feedback should be constructive. It might begin with a critical view, but should end with the pupil being aware of how he/she can move forward.

Speaking on a one-to-one basis is probably the most effective feedback situation because you can have a dialogue with the pupil, but it not always possible in the time available. Marking is a more traditional way of providing individual feedback. It is particularly useful when you have large classes and cannot speak to all individuals during the lesson time. It also allows you to respond to pupils from a distance (marking away from the classroom). Other forms of feedback include filling in competitive charts (e.g. spelling, learning tables, mental arithmetic, work cards) and rewards for competitive behaviour (e.g. smiley faces, house points, smarties in the jar). All these are extrinsic reward systems which assume the children appreciate the approval of others.

Pupils need to know how well they have done on tasks. Feedback should be given promptly. All written work should be responded to. Helpful comment should be made to pupils on the way they have tackled tasks as well as on what they have achieved. All comments should be positive or constructive so that pupils can improve their response.

Links

Communication about learning
Competition
Marking
Motivation
Rewards
Thinking skills

Strategies

- Ensure feedback is given promptly.
- Offering constructive comments in whole-class, group and individual situations.
- Through questioning, encourage pupils to explain their thinking and actions.
- Encourage pupils to decide what action needs to be taken.
- Setting up a reward system.
- Finding opportunities for others to reward with praise.
- Improve feedback within your marking system.

Development

Feedback, marking and reward are closely linked topics and need to be examined together, although one can be targeted while the others are maintained. In education, increasing value is being put on the quality and type of feedback. It is important that constructive feedback offers a balance to the increasing number of summative tests. Learning takes place more successfully when there is a dialogue between pupils and teacher and between pupils and their peers. Talking about what they understand so far about a topic often clarifies issues. The opportunity to reflect on and rectify errors is tremendously important because pupils make errors at the limits of their learning and they need to establish correct understanding.

Smith (2001) suggests that if children give themselves feedback about the tasks they are doing as they go along, then the learning will be more established and connected in their brains. This feedback could be a parallel account of what is happening but it could be reflective, linked to previous experience or making hypotheses, each of which is a powerful support for learning. The Assessment Reform Group (2002), which was begun with work by Black and Wiliam (1998) on assessment for learning, comment that, 'Teachers should be aware of the impact that comments, marks and grades can have on learners' confidence and enthusiasm and should be as constructive as possible in the feedback that they give'.

Further reading

Assessment Reform Group www.assessment-reform-group.org.uk

Black, P. and Wiliam, D. (1998) *Inside the Black Box: Raising Standards through Classroom Assessment*, London: School of Education.

Sangster, M. and Overall, L. (2006) *Assessment: A Practical Guide for Primary Teachers*, London: Continuum. Chapter 10 draws on various works to discuss feedback.

Smith, A. (2001) 'What the most recent brain research tells us about learning?', in Banks, F. and Shelton Mayes, A. (eds) *Early Professional Development for Teachers*, London: David Fulton/Open University.

TDA references

Q12, Q27, Q28.

Formative assessment (monitoring pupils' learning)

Most assessment in the classroom is formative, because teachers are trying to build on what the children know, and to sort out misconceptions. Formative assessment occurs in several 'time frames'. From minute to minute you will be making decisions in the light of pupils' responses, at the end of the lesson or day you will be assessing pupils' performance, your own teaching, and planning future action. Medium-term assessments and planning will also be part of the analysis which will feed into future planning.

A reasonable assessment expectation in an oral, whole-class situation is to note exceptionally good and exceptionally weak responses and get a general 'feel' for whole-class understanding. When working orally with the whole class there are very few situations where it is possible to assess everyone's understanding. Group work or written responses provide a greater opportunity to observe or monitor pupils' performance. A group objective is a closer match to individual children's ability and therefore progress is expected and more likely to occur. In some lessons it is possible for the teacher to focus on a group and collect useful data.

It might be that the same learning objective(s) are visited in several lessons, so it is easier to build a picture of the class over a short period of time. Also, the objective is often returned to in the medium term in the form of assessments such as problems and tests.

A teacher may choose to assess what children know and can do prior to running a topic so that he/she can set more meaningful objectives in medium- and short-term planning.

Assessments can be formal, such as tests and exams, or informal, such as talking and observing, but will be formative if you take action on the results. Formative assessments are a vital part of the cycle of effective teaching. They are used to inform your next planning and teaching as well as recording individual progress.

Links

Differentiation
Evaluating lessons
Feedback
Marking
Medium-term planning
Recording individual progress
Summative assessment
Target-setting

Strategies

- Observe and question children respond appropriately to their answers and level of understanding.
- Assess and act upon the learning that has and has not taken place in a lesson (recording and future planning).
- Select appropriate information to record informally and formally (consider purpose).
- Use formative assessment on your own teaching skills (self-evaluation).

Development

Assessment is used for many different purposes and therefore it is important that you select a form of assessment which provides you with the information you need. For a good summary of the purposes and principles of assessment refer to Harlen et al. in Pollard (1996: 264). For a more extensive view of formative assessment in the primary school refer to Sangster and Overall (2006). For earlier views of formative assessment which has now come to be known as 'assessment for learning' refer to the research of Black et al. (1998, 2004) and Clarke (2001, 2003).

Further reading

Black, P. and Wiliam, D. (1998) *Inside the Black Box: Raising Standards through Classroom Assessment,* London: School of Education.

Black, P., Harrison, C., Lee, C.,Marshall, B. and Wiliam, D. (2004) *Assessment for Learning: Putting It into Practice* Maidenhead: Open University Press.

Clarke, S. (2001) *Unlocking Formative Assessment,* London: Hodder and Stoughton.

Clarke, S. (2003) *Enriching Feedback in the Primary Classroom,* London: Hodder and Stoughton.

Harlen, W., Gipps, C., Broadfoot, P. and Nuttall, D. (1996) 'Assessment purposes and principles', in Pollard, A. (ed.) *Readings for Reflective Teaching in the Primary School,* London: Continuum.

Sangster, M. and Overall, L. (2006) *Assessment: A Practical Guide for Primary Teachers,* London: Continuum.

TDA references

Q12, Q13, Q27, Q28.

Foundation stage

The Foundation stage covers the age range three to five years in England and Wales. The curriculum for this age group in state schools is steered by two documents, *Curriculum Guidance for the Foundation Stage* (DfES/QCA, 2000) and the *Foundation Stage Profile* (QCA, 2003) which replaced Baseline Assessment in 2003. The CGFS has six areas of development.

- Personal, social and emotional development.
- Communication, language and literacy.
- Mathematical development.
- Knowledge and understanding of the world.
- Physical development.
- Creative development.

These are set out in three Steps which increase in expectation with the third Step related to the Early Learning Goals which indicate the level to be achieved by five year olds before they enter Key Stage 1. This is linked to the Foundation Stage Profile which has 13 summary scales covering the six areas of learning.

Links

Formative assessment
Play and structured learning
Research and its uses
Summative assessment

Strategies

- Make yourself familiar with the Curriculum Guidance for the Foundation stage.
- Make yourself familiar with the Foundation Stage Profile.
- Find out how the results are used.
- Use the Profile to plan new work for children.

Development

It is important that young children have a stimulating environment in which they can develop their creativity. Sometimes curricula can be interpreted too rigorously and children are subject to a series of goals which the teacher is keen for the children to meet. This needs to be turned on its head in the Foundation stage with the children at the centre and the curriculum responding to their knowledge and interests. The teacher needs to be well organized in providing a learning environment in which the child becomes engaged. The teacher and other adults are often the facilitator and children opt in and out of many activities. Play is of great value and can be structured or free. Children are nurtured rather than taught in a formal way. The adults will be collecting information about children's progress and recording this in an ongoing way within the Foundation Stage Profile. Future experiences will be structured around children's needs as well as providing a rich and varied curriculum.

Further reading

www.qca.org.uk/160.html
www.surestart.gov.uk

TDA reference

Q3(a, b).

Gender

Gender is as much about how we dress as it is about biological factors. To be seen as a man or a woman will be determined by the rules that a society has for these at a moment in time. Your experience of gender will be influenced by your up-bringing. It is also likely that your experience will be different to that experienced by those who brought you up. Your schooling, your friends and your experience of work all make your experience of being a man or a woman unique. In your teaching recognize that your uniqueness is both an advantage and a disadvantage. As a teacher you will have a set of expectations about the children you teach. Your gender, like your position in society and your race, raises expectations in the children you teach and in their parents and carers. The differences in attitudes between you and them may be considerable. Some children have learned from the home to disregard women. Some have learned to disregard men. It should be noted that achievement for girls in the UK seems to be outstripping that of boys at many stages. Your awareness about gender will inform your teaching as gender influences the way children behave and learn. Smith (2001: 120), quoting work by Moir and Jessell (1993) has a useful summary of the differences. These include:

- boys are better at spatial reasoning, girls are better at language
- girls talk before boys
- boys talk and play more with inanimate objects
- girls read character and social clues better
- girls talk their way through maths problems, boys work non-verbally
- girls are better at verbal activity, boys have better general maths ability
- boys need more space than girls
- boys have a shorter attention span.

These are, of course, generalizations. Many children will not conform to the stereotypes above. Nevertheless, knowing about these differences means that you can choose methods, resources and examples that will help your learners.

Links

Equal opportunities
Ethnicity
Learning styles
Research and its uses

Strategies

- Take account of gender differences in the way you teach.
- Use methods that stimulate both verbal and non-verbal learning.
- Use both visual aids and verbal instruction.
- Break learning into small steps, give opportunities to undertake whole tasks.
- Give tasks that demand an emotional response, role play, discussion and debate, 'how would you feel if...'.
- Aim for a balance of activities that appeal to girls and to boys.
- Get children to challenge their preferred ways of learning by doing tasks that make them feel less comfortable.

Further reading

Cole, M., Hill, D. and Shan, S. (eds) (1997) *Promoting Equality in Primary Schools*, London: Cassell.

Smith, A. (2001) 'The strategies that accelerate learning in the classroom', in Banks, F. and Shelton Mayes, A. (eds) (2001) *Early Professional Development for Teachers*, London: Open University/David Fulton.

TDA reference

Q18.

Group work

In many aspects of life we are required to work with others, so it is important that children learn how to cooperate with other children on tasks. Many school situations require individual learning and achievement and it is easy to overlook opportunities to work as a team and to work in different teams. It is interesting to see who takes the lead in group work, who has the ideas, who comes up with the solutions and who does the work leading to the presentation stage. With carefully structured groups, the teacher can foster these collaborative work skills. Problem solving is a good setting for group work, as is sport, drama and presentations.

Groups are often created in class to allow for differentiation of work. In this situation groups of like ability are placed together and provided with the same work. Even though they may be sitting round the same table, they may not be expected to work together. Mixed ability groups can also be used in appropriate situations. It is important for the teacher to decide which grouping is appropriate for the work which is to be done. Children's abilities may vary from subject to subject so there is a need to vary the way the groups are organized.

Links

Differentiation
Problem solving
Skills and strategies
Social development
Whole-class teaching

Strategies

- Plan opportunities for group work in appropriate settings.
- Organize groups as well as allowing for free choice on occasions.
- Use ability groups when work needs to be differentiated.
- Vary the groups according to the tasks.

Development

Looking more closely at group work in the large ORACLE survey carried out in 1980 (Galton et al.), it was observed that children were mainly set individual tasks when sitting in groups, that most comments made between group members were managerial, only nine per cent being intellectually stimulating exchanges.

McNamara (1996) visits some of the issues raised when ability groups are used, he comments that whole-class teaching is a more effective learning strategy and finally suggests that the desks be arranged in a horseshoe shape for maximum attention and flexibility.

Bennett et al. (1984), in their research into classroom practice, observed a great deal of whole-class teaching with the work aimed at the middle ability band with the set tasks being too easy or too difficult for half the pupils.

The social/academic benefits of legitimizing talk ought to help with establishing the task and in motivating children to complete their contribution, although sometimes the group dynamics are not always positive and the team pull in different directions.

Bennett and Dunne (1992) state there are three issues to be taken into account when planning cooperative group work: the interaction between social and cognitive intentions of the grouping; the type of task required; and the match or appropriateness of the task to the children in the group.

Further reading

Bennett, N. and Dunne, E. (1992) *Managing Classroom Groups*, Hemel Hempstead: Simon and Schuster.

Bennett, N., Desforges, C., Cockburn, A. and Wilkinson, B. (1984) *The Quality of Pupil Learning Experiences*, Hillsdale, N.J.: Erlbaum.

Galton, M., Simon, B. and Croll, P. (1980) *Inside the Primary Classroom*, London: Routledge and Kegan Paul.

McNamara, D. (1996) 'To group or not to group', in Pollard, A. (ed.) *Reading for Reflective Teaching in the Primary School*, London: Continuum.

TDA reference

Q25(a).

Harassment

See *Bullying*.

Homework and out-of-class work

There are varying practices in schools about issuing homework. At its most positive it should be seen as an opportunity to establish the practice of study in the home environment, hopefully with the support of others at home. It should be a vehicle for building independent learning. The content should be engaging and possibly relevant to the environment the children are working in. It should not rely on the provision of resources from home (an *Equal opportunities* issue). The amount should be reasonable within a set time limit and the homework should have a clear schedule so that parents and carers know what is expected and can therefore support your expectations. Completed work should be expected and encouragement and praise be given both at home and school. The work should also be seen or followed up in school to show that it is valued and makes a useful contribution to learning. It should be strongly linked to the learning taking place in school and the children should have a clear understanding of what they are expected to do.

Links

Equal opportunities
Independent learning

Strategies

- Be clear about the time to be spent on the homework.

- If possible, inform parents and carers of the homework schedule.
- Make sure the work is appropriate for the environment in which they will be working.
- Link the work to what is being learned in class.
- Expect the work to be completed, mark it or follow it up in class.
- Praise completion and good work.
- Try not to give finishing off as homework.
- If possible, choose something which the children find engaging to do.

Development

Parents and carers and schools have different viewpoints about homework. Some schools believe that their pupils need a large amount of independent study work. On the other hand, some parents and carers believe that academic work should be completed in school and home is for other leisure-type activities. From the pupils' viewpoint, life should be a balance between freedom of choice and study. There is also the question of how old should children be when they are first given homework?

Some schools discourage teachers from sending home 'finishing off' as they believe that either the teacher has not made a good judgement about the amount of work set or that allowing 'finishing off' encourages children to delay work until they get home.

Further discussion could be had on the type of work set. Do we need children to work through 20 examples or should they return prepared to discuss how they worked out one example? Is it possible to complete this particular work in that particular home environment? Some places have set up 'homework clubs' which children attend after school. This is particularly for children whose parents and carers are out at work or who do not have an easy home study environment.

Hayes (1999) offers useful discussion on aspects of homework, including what teachers need to consider when managing homework. He warns that it is time consuming and no substitute for actually teaching children. This leads back to what kinds of things we are asking children to do for homework and why. Muijs and Reynolds (2001) also have a useful and practical discussion on the effective use of homework.

Further reading

The DfES (England and Wales) have issued useful guidance on homework. It can be found on the Parents'
Centre website at www.parentscentre.gov.uk/educationandlearning/whatchildrenlearn/
learningathomeoutsideschool/homework

Hayes, D. (1999) *Planning Teaching and Class Management in Primary Schools*, London: David Fulton.

Muijs, D. and Reynolds, D. (2001) *Effective Teaching: Evidence and Practice*, London: Paul Chapman Publishing.

TDA reference

Q24.

Inclusion

The first thoughts about inclusion often go straight to pupils with special educational needs, but it is wider than this. It is about all pupils who are at risk of exclusion through:

- non-attendance – truancy, long-term illness, long holidays in term time
- disaffection – pupils who attend but take no interest in learning, pupils who bully and their victims
- formal exclusion – pupils whose conduct has been unacceptable in school through persistent defiance of legitimate school rules
- disadvantage – poverty, poor housing, nutrition, poor parenting, children 'looked after' by the state
- pupil mobility – travellers' children, asylum seekers, immigrants.

A social justice view of education takes the view that high quality education for all is an inclusive goal. Social justice has at its roots the idea that economic, racial and gender discrimination are not acceptable. It follows that action needs to be taken to ensure that everyone is able to be included. This implies that strong partnerships and working relationships are needed between parents and carers pupils, teachers and teaching assistants and the different agencies. In the UK, the aim is that mainstream schools should meet the needs of as many pupils as possible.

A useful concept when thinking about inclusion is that of *barriers to learning*. Prejudice and stereotyping are often significant in creating and maintaining these barriers. Pupils who are difficult to teach can evoke negative responses. Rather than thinking about what pupils can achieve we sometimes think of what they cannot do. The ways in which pupils are referred to often gives clues about the mindset of the speaker. For example, 'This is John, he has difficulty in seeing the print in most books so he uses large print books' has a more positive and therefore more inclusive feel, than saying, 'John is a partially sighted pupil' or 'a blind pupil'. Inclusion is about looking for ways of reducing the barriers to learning that exist for pupils who present more of a challenge to school staff.

Links

Differentiation
Equal opportunities
Expectations about pupils' learning
Special educational needs
Teaching in teams
Working with other adults

Strategies

Consider the ways you can reduce barriers to learning by:

- Looking for positive attributes in pupils who are difficult to teach.
- Praising any improvement – rewarding effort and celebrating achievement – e.g. be aware that sitting still for two minutes is a real achievement for some children!
- Being careful about the assumptions you make, e.g. hearing a noise behind you and blaming the 'normal culprit' when he or she is innocent can make it worthwhile for that pupil to misbehave in future. 'Mr X ain't fair, he's always picking on me' gives some pupils the excuse they need not to conform to the rules.
- Using teaching assistants effectively.
- Building your knowledge about the difficulties that cause some pupils to find learning in school difficult.

Development

Can social inclusion happen? Three ideas – social inclusion, educational inclusion and inclusive schools – are central to UK government policy, *Every Child Matters* (Children Act, 2004) makes this quite clear. Publicly funded schools in England through a rigorous inspection system have required teachers to get better at their work, i.e. to teach *every* pupil more effectively. This has been accompanied by many other measures to begin to enable much greater inter-agency cooperation. Educational inclusion, with the underlying ideas from social inclusion, is about meeting the different needs of as many pupils as possible in mainstream schooling. This happens in many ways. For example.

Many more teaching assistants are employed to work alongside teachers to support pupils. They work with individuals, groups and classes as part of a workplace reform agenda.

Schools have been asked to consider carefully all the ways they can keep pupils in school. Many schools have sought ways to encourage pupils to arrive on time and to be ready to learn, through things like breakfast clubs. Rewards for full week of attendance help to reduce unauthorized absence from school. Pupils with unacceptable behaviour, who are in danger of exclusion, may get extra support to keep them where they can continue school learning.

The idea of an inclusive school that will meet the needs of many pupils in a variety of ways; within special classes, through support for individuals, differentiation in the curriculum and carefully thought through teaching, is an exciting idea.

Further reading

Clough, P. and Corbett, J. (2000) *Theories of Inclusive Education: A Students' Guide*, London: Paul Chapman.
Lorenz, S. (2002) *First Steps in Inclusion*, London: David Fulton. This handbook has some excellent starting places for making the ideas of social justice work.
See these webpages for the most up-to-date information:
www.everychildmatters.gov.uk
inclusion.ngfl.gov.uk

TDA reference

Q1, Q2, Q10.

Independent learning

One of the hardest but most creditable achievements of a teacher is to help his or her pupils along the road to independent learning. Lots of things have to come together to achieve this goal. Pupils need to want to do good work and behave because they feel proud to conduct themselves in this way.

They have to learn to be decision makers. They have to become involved in the work because they want to do it, not because the teacher says all the time that they have to do it. They have to know what they want to achieve and therefore why they are doing the work. They should want to conduct themselves well around the classroom and to treat each other with respect, because it feels right to them.

As a teacher you need to give them opportunities to exercise these choices, but it will not happen if you just remove all the structures and discipline. Self-discipline comes through recognizing what discipline is. The teacher creates order and gradually encourages more independent decision making through discussion and guidance. There may be 'whole class' stages of this progression or, existing side-by-side, individuals who are ready to take on more responsibility. You, as the teacher, must decide who is ready for 'the greater freedom'. This aligns with the ideas about personalized learning.

Links

Active learning
Discipline
Expectations about pupils' learning
Motivation
Problem solving
Self-assessment by pupils
Skills and strategies

Strategies

- Find ways of allowing responsible pupils to be more involved in decisions about their work.
- Discuss expected behaviour and work outputs with the whole class.
- Be clear about why pupils are doing particular pieces of work (purpose as well as objective) (personalize the learning).
- Ensure certain resources are accessible without permission and, if appropriate, there are choices about what to use.
- Try to make sure all decision making does not have to pass through you.
- In suitable situations allow pupils to help each other.

Development

Encouraging children to be independent learners is a long-term goal. It is not easy to achieve and you as a teacher will need to think carefully about the 'campaign'. Some children enjoy working at projects and are happy to do so on their own. They always seem to be motivated and engage in anything you offer. Initially, many other children will sit there waiting for you to tell them what to do next. Most children are very teacher dependent. Some teachers like their pupils to be like this, as it offers strong control and they are happy for this to be the status quo for all the year. While control is vital, over and above that, self-control by pupils is even better. If you leave the room will the children continue to work? To achieve this, the pupils need to be able to operate independently of the teacher. This is achieved by promoting a range of skills and understanding. Children need to be confident about their own decision making, they need to be skilled at selecting and using information, they need to know the purpose of the task, they need to want to engage in the task and they need to have work to move on to if they complete the task early. These are just a few of the opportunities that have to be regularly promoted and praised throughout the year if you want children to manage their own work.

Further reading

Moyles, J. and Robinson, G. *Beginning Teaching: Beginning Learning in Primary Education* (2nd edn), Buckingham: Open University.

More about personalized learning can be found at:
www.standards.dfes.gov.uk/personalisedlearning

TDA reference

Q19, Q24, Q25(d).

Instruction

Letting pupils know that you're ready to start has to be one of the first things you'll learn to do. You'll need a procedure for gaining everyone's undivided attention. In large spaces two hand claps is a good way of getting attention without shouting. Your instructions need to be brief, clear and positive. Your tone needs to be confident and pleasant. Often you'll need to reinforce your instruction by rephrasing and directing your comments to particular pupils. For example,

> (*Teacher claps twice.*) 'Can I have everyone's attention, thanks. Martin, Abdul, Shahida and Susan, look this way, thanks. Now, when I tell you, I want one person from each group to collect the apparatus from me. Everyone else in the group needs to clear away anything that's on your table that's not needed for the experiment. Is that clear? (*Teacher waits for nods and other indications that the instruction is clear, by scanning each table in turn.*) One set of apparatus and one prepared table. Off you go.'

Give generalized instructions once, for example, 'Everyone start work now'. Follow this up by telling a particular child what you want, 'John, start work now'. For some learners two or three instructions overloads the memory, this may mean that they seem not to be doing what you have asked. One instruction at a time helps them all remember what you want them to do. Don't nag by giving the same instruction to everyone over and over again; this stops pupils listening the first time. Acknowledge those who have heeded your instructions with a smile, a gesture and some quiet praise.

You'll also be preparing worksheets and other written material which instructs pupils to do something. You'll need to know how best to do this for the whole range of ability. Keeping the language simple, sentences short and being really clear is the key. You may have to prepare two or three versions before you get this right, trialling them with pupils who you know find reading instructions hard. Even then you'll have the instructions read to some pupils. Another pupil may do this or you might use a taped version or a teaching assistant.

Links

Communicating clearly
Communication about learning
Demonstration by the teacher
Discipline
Expectations about pupils' learning
Explaining
Independent learning
Purposeful working atmosphere
Relationships with pupils
Timing within lessons
Transitions
Whole-class teaching
Working with parents and carers, professionals and other adults

Strategies

When instructing pupils:
- Have a clear signal that gets everyone's attention.
- Be pleasant and confident, stand still, get eye contact, smile, use a clear tone of voice.
- Be precise, be clear yourself what you want done and how it is to be done.
- Be brief.
- Be positive, for example, use 'thanks' rather than 'please'. ('Thanks' often demonstrates that you are confident that your instruction will be followed; 'please' can have a pleading quality.)
- Reinforce the instruction through repeating it.
- Deal separately with anyone who has not yet complied.
- Quiet praise to individuals who do as they are asked promptly helps to build a positive working atmosphere.
- Written instructions for your teaching need to be kept simple:
  i   by using direct language, avoid negatives, explain technical terms
  ii use short sentences, avoid 'it' or 'they', repeat the subject, (e.g. most pupils will find 'The cats woke up. The cats went out.' easier to read than 'The cats woke up. They went out.')

    iii use a clear type face (Arial is a good example, and at least 12 point)

    iv use a straightforward layout.

- Check that your written instructions have been understood by pupils.
- Be prepared to trial written instructions to get them to a level that most pupils can read.
- Pupils who find reading hard should have appropriate additional help.

Development

Some instructions are to do with class management. They make the day-to-day organization of the minutiae of teaching and learning possible. Instructions are also part of lesson planning. Both are part of making learning easier. However, you'll also want to consider how you encourage pupils to make decisions about how, when and where to do things as independent learners.

Further reading

Moyles, J. and Robinson, G. (eds) (2002) *Beginning Teaching: Beginning Learning in Primary Education*, (2nd edn), Buckingham: Open University.

TDA reference

Q25(c).

Intellectual development

How we learn is a focus of development studies. Development theorists have different, but often complementary, ideas about intellectual growth. Behaviourists, however, offer another idea. There are four theories which you should know about.

The *behaviourist theories* (from the 1920s onwards, with psychologists Pavlov, Skinner and Bandura as the more important names) emphasized change in behaviour as the outcome of learning. The stimulus–response model is clearly seen in much direct instruction, including the management of behaviour.

Jean Piaget's theory of *cognitive development* has two essential elements. He suggests that our minds actively seek to make sense of the world. Our cognitive structures (our minds) are *adaptations* which take knowledge and make it fit with the world about us. He studied many pre-school children. His observations about the mistakes that they make, their misunderstandings which arose from their point of view about how things work, lead him to suggest that 'cognitive development is a process of revision: children revise their knowledge to provide an increasingly better fit to reality' (Keenan, 2002: 37). His second big idea was to suggest that we move through four stages. The knowledge structures used by learners are relatively similar and stable throughout each stage. At the *sensorimotor stage,* birth to about two years, 'the infant thinks about the world through their actions on it' (Keenan, 2002: 37). The random actions of the child become increasingly more organized and systematic. The child becomes more able to handle abstract ideas and moves into *preoperational stage,* two to seven years. At this stage the child becomes able to handle thinking through symbolic representation. In the concrete operational stage, seven to 12 years, logical thought becomes well established. The *formal operational stage,* adolescence, sees the development of abstract thought. These days this influential theory is increasingly criticized. You'll discover that the child as a solitary learner has little or no support these days.

Lev Vygotsky's *sociocultural theory of development* also sees children as active explorers of the world in which they find themselves. He suggested that it is the social interactions with the people that children meet that make it possible for learning to happen. He also believed that there is a pattern to the development, that children move from working with others, to working things out for themselves, characterized by self-talk where the child will talk him/herself through a task. He also observed that parents and teachers, when working with children, tailored what they said, the way they said it and what they did to support the child's development. You will find this referred to as 'scaffolding'.

Information processing models and theories seem, after an uncertain start, are really useful. These arise from computer modelling. *Connectionist* models that match brain-function to learning tasks seem promising. For example, the use of advanced organizers to help to make connections between what the child already knows and what has to be learned, is one aspect of this theory in classroom use.

All these theories and models have something to offer teachers. It would be impossible to think about teaching and learning without them. Many teachers confirm that children do move through stages. We think of our pupils as active and engaged learners. We know that the interventions we make can help or hinder learning and we are beginning to understand how knowledge of the physiology of the brain can help. Clearly this is the briefest of brief outlines; you'll want to learn more.

Links

Active learning

Differentiation
Discipline
Independent learning
Intervention
Linguistic development
Research and its uses
Social development
Thinking skills

Further reading

Keenan, T. (2002) *An Introduction to Child Development*, London: Sage.

Muijs, D. and Reynolds, D. (2005) *Effective Teaching: Evidence and Practice* (2nd edn), London: Paul Chapman.

Overall, L. S. (2007) *Supporting Children's Learning*, London: Sage.

Smith, P. K., Cowie, H. and Blades, M. (2003) *Understanding Children's Development* (4th edn), Oxford: Blackwell.

Sousa, D. A. (2001) *How the Brain Learns* (2nd edn), Thousand Oaks: Corwin, is recommended for a straightforward introduction to the brain.

TDA reference

Q18.

Intervention

Intervention is when the teacher engages with groups or individuals in an attempt to move them on with the work they are doing. The most successful interventions enable children to extend their thinking. These usually come in the form of questioning, prompts and requests for explanations from the pupils. Try not to give immediate solutions. It is deflating and demotivating. The children will not develop their problem-solving skills if everything is too easy or straightforward. We need children to develop their process skills and take ownership of the work they do.

Intervention can also be considered in the context of behaviour. Much poor behaviour can be prevented by an early intervention into a deteriorating situation. As you get to know a class there will be clues as to the way things are going. For example, a change in the type of noise, known offenders getting restless, or children disengaged from the task because it is too hard. If you sense anything like this, act upon it quickly. If possible do not let the situation deteriorate to the point where you get into disciplinary routines.

Links

Discipline
Group work
Independent learning
Linguistic development
Listening and responding to pupils
Play and structured learning
Questioning

Strategies

- Decide or explore with a child how much help they really need.
- Try to promote children thinking for themselves by choosing a prompt or question type of intervention.
- Try to anticipate problems by early intervention.
- Spot check on children most likely to misbehave (make them aware you are keeping an eye on them).

Development

Lev Vygotsky (1991), a Russian writer and educationalist who lived in the first half of the twentieth century, developed a theory known as the 'zone of proximal development' (ZPD). This term describes the influence the teacher has when working with a child. The greater the improvement when working with the teacher as opposed to the child working on his/her own, the greater the zone of proximal development, which, Vygotsky thought, was an indicator of potential learning power. An example of this would be an able child dramatically extending and expressing their understanding due to the teacher's intervention with questioning and prompts.

'Scaffolding' is the current term used to describe teacher intervention to support learning. It is the provision of structures by the teacher to enable learning to take place. This might be light touch such as introducing a task, giving verbal prompts as the task unfolds, or more strongly structured intervention such as a demonstration of the procedure to be followed. Over time a teacher might remove the 'scaffolding' as he/she feels the concept is established. One can see how scaffolding has close links to Vygotsky's zone of proximal development. Mercer and Dawes (2001) researched how teacher and pupil–pupil language supports learning. They draw upon the theories of Vygotsky and scaffolding to illuminate the dialogues which take place in the classroom.

Wood and Middleton (1975) studied pre-school mothers supporting the play of their 4 year olds. They observed that there were varying degrees of intervention which they moved between, depending on whether their child was stuck in their problem solving or not. Full support was a demonstration, a lighter touch was arranging the materials for assembly, then pointing out the relevant instruction and, lightest of all, giving general verbal prompts. It would be interesting to review what types of intervention are practised in the primary school. It is possible that there are strong parallels with the findings of Wood and Middleton.

Further reading

Mercer, N. and Dawes, L. (2001) 'Dialogues for teaching and learning', in Banks, F. and Shelton Mayes, A. (eds) *Early Professional Development for Teachers*, London: David Fulton/Open University.

Vygotsky, L. (1991) *Thought and Language* (translation edited Kuzulin, A.), Cambridge, MA: MIT Press.

Wood, D. and Middleton, D. (1975) 'A study of assisted problem-solving', *British Journal of Psychology*, 66: 2, 181–91.

TDA references

Q19, Q25(a).

Learning objectives

When planning in the medium- and the short-term it is important to identify what you want children to know and be able to do. A learning objective can be about gaining a new piece of knowledge or acquiring a new skill. The objective of the lesson might be to consolidate or assess a piece of learning. Learning objectives for a lesson might start with the words:

> to introduce . . .   to be able to . . .   to practise . . .   to apply . . .
> to revise . . .   to assess understanding of . . .

They are all focused on what the expected outcome for the pupils is, and involve a process of learning rather than stating the completion of a particular task. The tasks used are the vehicles for the learning. For example, 'to introduce multiplying by 3' is a learning objective as opposed to 'constructing block towers in threes' which does not state what mathematical learning will take place. Some lessons have sub-objectives within the group task phase of the lesson. This allows for differentiation to take place.

Once you have a clear and manageable objective, the planning and teaching become easier and more focused. The assessment becomes easier too, as you know what you are looking for in the children's performance. It is probable that the assessment criterion for the lesson is similar to the learning objective, or is a part of it. It could be appropriate to record whether particular children have met your objective. Certainly it is appropriate for you, as teacher, to evaluate whether the class and groups have met objectives so that you can feed this into your planning (see *Evaluating lessons*). In practice this will mean that you draw from both your scheme and records to plan a follow-on lesson.

Links

Active learning
Differentiation
Evaluating lessons
Formative assessment
Foundation stage
Lesson plan structure
Medium-term planning
Primary National Strategy

Strategies

- Use sub-objectives, if necessary, to differentiate work.
- Choose an objective that describes the required learning rather than the task.
- Make the objective reasonably achievable within one or two lessons.
- Plan objectives that build on previous learning.
- Have a cycle of introduction, consolidation and application rather than a new objective each lesson.
- Link learning objectives to assessment criteria.

Development

Children are more likely to learn if your objective is clear and manageable and the purpose is clear to them. Both of these need to be made explicit at the start of the lesson. Some would advocate writing the objective on the board. It depends on whether you think this is an effective strategy for the pupils you teach. Some teachers share their objectives with the parents and carers of their pupils.

A series of carefully constructed objectives should lead to progression in learning and will provide strong evidence for inspection in medium- and short-term planning. You will have to make decisions about worthwhile diversions from your original planning. Maybe the children failed to grasp your objective and you want to revisit it the next day. Maybe a really interesting aspect developed and you feel the children will learn much by pursuing it. Maybe an event occurred or a child brought a fascinating object into school. These spontaneous situations are no less valid than your planned programme. Evaluate what the children will gain from a change of programme. It is usually a positive learning experience. Just not the one you planned.

TDA references

Q22, Q26(b).

Learning styles

You'll know that your preferred way of learning is unique. No one else learns in quite the same way as you do. The same as each child you teach will have a preferred way of learning. Our challenge is to match our teaching to the variety of learning styles[1] that our children may have. And, as far as we can, to give them access to all the learning styles and strategies that they may need to use.

Our five senses give us information about the world, but they don't all contribute equally to the way we learn. We may have a preference to learn visually (perhaps you doodle) – *visual learners*; or through listening – *auditory learners*; or you may prefer touch or whole body movement – *kinaesthetic learners*. Whichever, sensory preferences are important in individual's learning. Using *VAK* (visual, auditory, kinaesthetic) delivery in balance in our teaching may not be research based, but it does seem to be a really helpful thing to do.

VAK teaching uses:

- Development of visual learning: text plus illustration, graph, maps, visualization to improve memory, access to CD-Roms, DVD, posters, keywords, video, demonstration, memory mapping (e.g. flow charts, story boards).
- Development of auditory learning: opportunities to talk about the work, lectures, i.e. something to listen to (radio or from CD and audio tape) to get the picture, spelling that recalls the pattern through sounds.
- Enablement of learning through movement (kinaesthetic), the opportunity to be active, role plays, field trips, hand and gestures when talking, demonstrations.

---

[1] Authors use slightly different terms for what is essentially the same idea, for example, learning strategies, cognitive style or strategy, or style constructs. It may be helpful to think about style as what we are born with and strategy as learned.

Links

Active learning
Differentiation
Displays
Intellectual development
Problem solving
Resources
Thinking skills

Strategies

- Recognizing different learning style means acknowledging that children will behave differently in lessons, e.g. kinaesthetic learners may seem to fidget more, they need to be active in order to learn. This knowledge can help to explain apparent misbehaviour, the restlessness you see may not be misbehaviour.
- Observe how children react to the different learning styles you use so that you can extend their ability to learn from each.
- Note that your own learning style preference is likely to be the way you teach. Take account of this when planning by deliberately using other styles in your teaching.
- Help children to recognize that they need to develop different learning strategies through exploring and talking about these with them.

Development

This idea of cognitive styles linked to preferred ways of learning feels right, but the research base is not strong. Riding and Rayner (1998: 9) after an extensive review of the literature suggest two learning styles, wholistic – analytic dimension; and verbal – imagery dimension; as valid. *Wholistic – analytic* individuals tend to organize information in wholes or parts. In a *verbal – imagery* style individuals tend to represent information through thinking verbally or in mental pictures.

Gardner (1983) in his analysis recognizes different kinds of intelligence; obvious ones are those of music or maths, but what about the people who are sensitive to the needs of others? *Multiple Intelligences* is an attractive theory as it suggests that human beings are problem solvers bringing different ways of thinking to different tasks. Particularly in the USA, his work influences the ways that teaching and learning are designed from nursery to higher education. Children and young people are encouraged to recognize and develop their particular intelligence. Teachers and teaching teams who understand Gardner, while allowing for particular talents, also encourage children to achieve their potential.

Further reading

Gardner, H. (1983, 1993) *Frames of Mind: The Theory of Multiple Intelligence*, New York: Basic Books. The second edition was published in Britain by Fontana Press.

Riding, R. (2002) *School Learning and Cognitive Style*, London: David Fulton. An authoritative and practical book that covers this area well.

Riding, R. and Rayner, S. (1998) *Cognitive Styles and Learning Strategies: Understanding Style Differences in Learning and Behaviour*, London: David Fulton.

Wikipedia at en.wikipedia.org/wiki/Learning_style has some excellent links for these ideas, try the link to Howard Gardner for more ideas about *multiple intelligences.*

TDA reference

Q19.

Lesson plan structure

The lesson plan is the document on which the detailed organization of your lesson is placed. You will transfer some of your headings from the medium-term planning and you will be making decisions about timing, exact content and resources. Whatever format you use, your lesson plan headings support your thinking on:

- what you want the children to achieve during the lesson (learning objective)
- what you are going to observe and assess (assessment criteria)
- how long you are going to spend on each part of the lesson (timing)
- how and when you are going to group the children (grouping)
- what organization you are going to use (organization)
- what resources you are going to need (resources)
- the specific nature of the content (content)
- prompts for the teaching points you are going to make (teaching points).

It is also a good strategy to have an extension activity for the speedy workers in your class. The plenary or conclusion is where you draw your lesson together and re-establish the objectives so that children know what they have to learn.

It is useful to have the lesson plan within reach during the lesson as a prompt. Putting the lesson plan in a transparent plastic folder will help in keeping it clean and easy to read.

In England the literacy and mathematics lessons have a specified structure, as suggested in the *National Literacy Strategy* (DES, 1998) and the *National Numeracy Strategy* (DES, 1999).

Links

Communicating clearly
Communicating about learning
Evaluating lessons
Explaining
Foundation stage
Group work
Instruction
Learning objectives
Long-term planning
Medium-term planning
Pace
Primary National strategy
Transitions
Whole-class teaching

Strategies

- Always prepare lesson plans so that you are clear and purposeful in your teaching.
- Keep to your proposed timing unless you have an educationally valid reason for adjusting it.
- Make the objective clear to the pupils at the start of the lesson and then return to the expected learning objective at the end.
- Keep your notes brief and easy to read, possibly using bullet points and a highlighter.
- Maintain an assessment focus throughout the lesson.

Development

Muijs and Reynolds (2001) describe two types of lesson: direct instruction and interactive. A piece of learning might go through stages over a series of lessons, and this is reflected in the balance of teacher input to pupils involved in task activities. This will be reflected in the timing and content of the lesson. Many people follow a three-part model which starts with whole-class teaching, moves on to group work, and then returns at the end to whole-class teaching. The first part of this often involves a review of previously taught connected work. The Numeracy and Literacy Strategies both have this mix of whole-class teaching and group work.

The structure of most lessons will require you to consider and plan for the following:

- learning objective
- assessment criteria and mode
- content
- organization (grouping, timing and resources)
- extension activities
- conclusion/plenary
- evaluation.

In addition to planning what the children will be doing, it is important to decide where you will be in the lesson and what you will be doing. This is particularly relevant during the group work where it is possible to spend the whole time 'policing' the classroom when you could be offering teaching input for part of the time. However detailed your planning there will always be differences in the speed at which pupils work, therefore it is important to plan how you will deal productively with the early finishers and those who do not complete their work.

Interesting variations on planning can be found in early years' work. Two good examples of different approaches can be found within the High/Scope and Reggio Emilia projects.

Further reading

Department for Education and Science (DES) (1998) *The National Literacy Strategy*, London: DfES.

Department for Education and Science (DES) (1999) *The National Numeracy Strategy*, London: DfES.

High Scope at www.highscope.org

Muijs, D. and Reynolds, D. (2001) *Effective Teaching: Evidence and Practice*, London: Paul Chapman Publishing.

Reggio Emilia at ceep.crc.uiuc.edu/eecearchive/digests/2000/new00.html

TDA reference

Q25.

Level descriptions

Level descriptions can be found in the assessment section of the English National Curriculum (see DfES website).

They are descriptions of pupils attainment within each of the attainment targets of the National Curriculum. In assessing the level of a child's perfor-mance, a best fit is made of their achievements against the descriptions provided. These descriptions are drawn from the Programmes of Study (syllabus). It is anticipated that the average seven year old in England and Wales should achieve a Level 2 and the average 11 year old a Level 4.

Level descriptions can be used by schools as part of their internal assessment strategies and reporting requirements, but nationally the children are assessed against these descriptions at the end of Key Stage 1 in English and mathematics, and in English, mathematics and science at the end of Key Stage 2. Wales no longer has tests for seven year olds. Teacher assessments at these stages must be reported to parents and carers alongside the results of the National Tests.

Links

Foundation stage
Primary National Strategy
Summative assessment

Strategies

- Match a pupil's work to the National Curriculum levels.
- Ensure individual records provide sufficient information to allow a National Curriculum level to be provided in each attainment target.
- Find out what teacher assessment is required during the year and set up assessment and recording systems to evidence this.

Development

Assessing children in this summative fashion on a national scale gives parents and carers, pupils and teachers an indication of their child's performance in relation to all the other children of his or her age in the whole country. From the school's point of view, the performance of pupils in their school provides feedback on how well the school is performing.

It is important for teachers to realize that tests sample a child's knowledge. 'Best fit' assessment indicates that the child is secure in a majority of the criteria but not necessarily all. Teachers' records kept against achievement (criterion-referenced procedures) will probably provide the most accurate picture of what a child does and does not know. Even then it is impossible for a teacher to establish exactly what a child knows at any one time.

Further reading

www.standards.dfes.gov.uk
QCA website for tests at www.qca.org.uk/ca/tests

TDA reference

Q11, Q26(a).

Linguistic development

The response of the babies to the pitch, rhythm and cadence of their mothers' voice, not the words, is observed from birth. Between 10–12 months the brain has become familiar with and is able to discriminate the separate sounds (phonemes) of the first language (the one the child hears at home). At about the same time babies begin to attach meaning to words. Speech, producing at first single words, may also start at this time. Learning grammar takes a little longer. Unfortunately, English grammar has many non-standard forms. Many two and three year olds are about 90 per cent correct, but many may still be learning, through the parents' correction, that, for example, 'I hitted (sic) it' needs to be 'I hit it'. The implication is that a language-rich pre-school life will advantage children.

The normal development pattern shows the following milestones:

- At birth babies *cry* to indicate distress, very soon these cries change, the caregiver is able to tell 'contented' or 'playful' cries from other cries.
- Between one to six months babies hear at first consonant sounds and slightly later vowel sounds. *Cooing* becomes *babbling*. They respond to the child-directed speech, *parentese*, that parents and carers give.
- Six–12 months babbling begins to be like speech, it gradually sounds like the infant's native language.
- Between 12–18 months single words – 'mama', 'dada' – come. The infant will point – *gesture* – and use a word to get what he/she wants, which is a one-word sentence.
- Somewhere between 18–24 months there is a great deal of naming, lots of new words are learned very fast, two-word sentences 'uh uh', 'all gone' – words in the correct order but without the function words – appear.
- Two and three year olds are learning really quickly through making many mistakes (over generalizations are very common) that parents and carers correct. Three-word sentences appear. Infants learn to take part in conversations.
- Up to about five years, gradually grammar and syntax (the order of words) become more complex. For example, the question form begins to be mastered. Infants will change how they speak in response to different contexts – home and out-of-the-home speech is heard.
- Beyond five to adolescence the number of words increases to 30,000, grammatical construction becomes more complex and, generally, the understanding and use of the full range of language use – things like *pronoun reference*, *metaphor*, *sarcasm* – become established.

Learning to read and write, unlike learning to speak, is not a 'natural' process. Most children have to be taught to read and write. The brain has to learn that marks on the page have meaning. The text is close to speech but not entirely the same. One important difference is the relative permanence of print. It can be read and reread. Learning to read and write in English with its complex alphabetic structure means learning about exceptions as well as rules. There are 44 phonemes, but only 26 letters. Listen to the sound of *o* in these words: *o*ne, w*o*men, wh*o*, T*o*m, the same letter can represent more than one sound. Then some sounds (phonemes) can be spelled in different ways, try these, b*y*, t*ie*, b*ye*, h*igh* – all ways of representing *i*. Another potential learning trap is in a word like 'cat' which sounds like one phoneme even though it is made up of three phonemes *c/ a/t*. Poor readers have difficulty with these principles. With instruction most children have begun to read well by the age of eight. Writing sometimes lags behind this. There are considerable differences in skill levels between pupils of the same age.

Links

Differentiation
English as an additional language
Gender
Intellectual development
Research and its uses
Social development

Further reading

Keenan, T. (2002) *An Introduction to Child Development*, London: Sage. Chapter 7 'The Development of Language and Communication' is recommended for understanding speech and listening.

Meece, J. L. (1997) *Child and Adolescent Development for Educators*, New York: McGraw Hill. Chapter 5 'Language Development and Literacy' is comprehensive.

Muijs, D. and Reynolds, D. (2005) *Effective Teaching: Evidence and Practice* (2nd edn), London: Paul Chapman. 'Literacy' Chapter 15, is an excellent summary on approaches to reading.

TDA reference

Q18.

Listening and responding to pupils

The classroom is a place where two worlds meet, the world of education and the world of home. As teachers we need to create opportunities for children to link both environments and contribute from their experience.

By listening and conversing with pupils they will feel valued and more likely to contribute. If you have developed good dialogue with individuals you will have also created a good setting for learning to take place.

There is a difference between making friends with children and establishing a good working relationship. In a good working relationship there is a two-way flow of ideas but the authority of the teacher is maintained at all times. The child will respond better to learning if he/she senses you are interested in his/her contributions. At the same time you will need to convey the boundaries of acceptable comment and behaviour to you as teacher. In this way the child will be aware and respect the rules of the relationship. You too must keep to these rules. See *Relationships with pupils* for further explanation.

Links

Communicating clearly
Communication about learning
Culture
Ethnicity
Misconceptions and remedies
Questioning
Relationships with pupils

Strategies

- Create opportunities for pupils to contribute from their own experiences.
- Make time to listen to pupils formally and informally.
- Be interested in children as people as well as in their work.
- Initiate dialogue about what they find hard or easy about work and respond to their comments.
- Develop listening skills with pupils.

Development

Pollard (1997) offers an interesting analysis of the way teachers and pupils communicate in the classroom. He points out that in 1980 as part of the Oracle project, infant children spent 12 per cent of their day listening to and interacting with the teacher. At the time of the PACE project in 1994, this had risen to 40 per cent. In classrooms where Literacy and Numeracy Strategies dominate the curriculum there is a good chance that the whole-class teaching element has pushed this figure even higher. This means that it is very important that communication is successful in the whole-class teaching phase of a lesson. It not only involves the teacher communicating clearly with the pupils, but it also involves both teacher and pupil in listening and responding. It is very common for the teacher to ask a question, a pupil to respond and then the teacher closes it down with an approving or disapproving remark. This is hardly the structure of genuine discussion and yet this question and answer routine is often claimed to be just that.

Pollard et al. (2005) identify four forms of listening, interactive, reactive, discriminative and appreciative. The interactive is the genuine discussion, the reactive, a response to instruction, the discriminative a listening skill to distinguish sounds and the appreciative where the listening is for enjoyment such as hearing stories, music and poetry. What balance of these occur in your classroom?

Further reading

Pollard, A. (1997) *Reflective Teaching in the Primary School* (3rd edn), London: Cassell.

Pollard, A. with Collins, J., Maddock, M., Simco, N., Swaffield, S., Warin, J. and Warwick, P. (2005) *Reflective Teaching: Evidence-informed Professional Practice* (2nd edn), London: Continuum.

TDA references

Q4, Q27, Q28.

Literacy, numeracy and ICT (Information and Communication Technology)

Both literacy, that is reading, writing, listening and speaking, and numeracy, that is understanding and using maths, are central to learning both in school and beyond. ICT is playing an increasing role as society becomes more computer literate and dependent on technology in work and leisure activities. All your planning and delivery for learning will need to include appropriate opportunities for learners to use and develop these. Literacy, numeracy and ICT are used across the curriculum.

Teaching literacy and numeracy and ICT through subjects is clearly a sensible thing to do; after all, each subject has its own demands. Sometimes these are subject specific, think of reading a map, a picture or watching a film. Sometimes, often, they will be more general. In all subjects learners need to be able to express ideas clearly and their critical thinking orally and in writing. Talking about the processes, concepts, ideas and facts of subjects will often precede reading and writing tasks. Similarly subjects will have specific numeracy demands.

In school there are two strands of technology use. The first is using ICT to support the organization and quality outputs in managing your teaching. The second is using ICT with learners to support a range of subject learning and to develop their ICT skills.

Your teaching can be supported by using literacy, numeracy and ICT to:

- plan medium-term (and short-term) documents
- create and record assessments
- prepare teaching materials
- prepare display materials
- access literacy, numeracy and ICT initiatives and information.

Working with pupils, literacy, numeracy and ICT can be used to:

- enhance subject learning through use of literacy and numeracy resources including ICT hardware, software and the internet
- develop pupils' literacy, numeracy and ICT skills through learning experiences.

When working with pupils you may be using one computer in the classroom with or without an electronic whiteboard, a suite of computers in a special room or a class set of mobile computers. You need to consider carefully the organization of each of these situations to get the most from them.

ICT encompasses a range of hardware, including interactive whiteboard, DVD/video, computer, overhead and/or data projector, tape players and recorder, program controlled toys (e.g. Roamer), all of which can be utilized effectively in the classroom in appropriately planned contexts.

Links

Lesson plan structure
Medium-term planning
Resources

Strategies

- Plan literacy, numeracy and ICT use into your lessons at the medium-term planning stage.
- When working in an ICT suite, structure your lesson, have a clear objective and a teaching input.
- When using one computer in the classroom select relevant programs and carefully organize how children will get a turn. Use some children to support skill learning and program instructions so you can be free to teach others.
- Use one computer and if possible an interactive whiteboard as a whole-class teaching aid.
- Provide a range of literacy, numeracy and ICT experiences.
- Use specific ICT lessons to promote skills.
- Use literacy, numeracy and ICT within lessons to promote subject learning.
- Check that all ICT hard and software works before the children arrive.
- Have explored for yourself the ICT programs you are going to use with the children.

Development

With the increase of computer accessibility, particularly to the world wide web and its vast stores of information, we will be forced to reassess our teaching approach to knowledge and the balance between knowledge and skills. A further issue is raised when we ask who has access to computers at home. Will the lack of computer access disadvantage some pupils? Will schools provide after-school access in the same way they are beginning to provide homework clubs?

A further interesting aspect of computer use by pupils is the programs they use. What do they learn from them? Does computer use encourage independent study? Do certain programs promote thinking skills? It is important to consider the purpose of a program when you plan to use it in class, in exactly the same way you decide about other activities you ask children to do. Even in school multimedia is increasingly important in its own right. Learners work on screen both to find information and ideas and produce multimedia text. Exciting software enables even the youngest to create webpages, computer graphics, video and similar computer-based applications. There are many types of programs including, games, information giving, practice and problem solving.

Trainee students' own competence in literacy, numeracy and ICT is tested prior to the award of QTS. Teachers and teaching assistants must know how to teach literacy, numeracy and ICT. They must also know how to use literacy, numeracy and ICT to teach their subject and to support their wider professional role.

Further reading

Often the best coverage of these issues is on websites, here are some:

www.bbc.co.uk/schools BBC Education is useful for internet resources.

www.becta.org.uk BECTa is the site for educational uses of ICT.

www.qca.org.uk QCA site is a useful site for schemes of work.

www.teachernet gov.uk Teachernet is a teacher resource and staff professional development site, including research for literacy, numeracy and ICT.

www.thereviewproject.org This site provides access to results of a two-year project on interactive whiteboards.

TDA references

Q16, Q17, Q23.

Long-term planning

Long-term planning is the allocation of topics throughout the year for each subject. It is carried out in schools to ensure coverage of legal curricula. Planning in this way will ensure that children in different classes in the same year group get an equable programme and it should help with progression of the curriculum from year to year.

If long-term planning is not in place then you need to consult with colleagues and coordinators to establish what progression is expected. It is useful to outline your intentions for the year so that you can get a sense of pace and begin to allocate groups of lessons. At this point you will probably move on to medium-term planning. It will be likely that you can use the same long-term structure, with minor adjustments, the following year.

The Primary National Strategy has recommended structures for long-term planning.

Links

Foundation stage

Medium-term planning

Primary National Strategy

Teaching in teams

Strategies

- Discuss long-term requirements with colleagues and coordinators.
- Establish what you are required to cover throughout the year.
- Apportion the topics into half-term blocks.
- Use this outline to develop medium-term plans.

Development

Structured content varies enormously from country to country, but there is remarkable similarity of goals in most curricula. An example of a very prescribed curriculum is that legally required in England, The National Curriculum, which has programmes of study for five to 16 year olds and expected outcomes, attainment targets, arranged into ten levels of achievement. Additionally at Key Stages 1, 2 and 3 (five years to 14 years) there are tests to measure individual and school attainment (see *Summative assessment* and QCA website).

Coherent long-term planning is dependent on a whole-school approach. This ensures a degree of progression for pupils. No more butterfly paintings in every year for the purpose of demonstrating reflective symmetry! With a prescribed curriculum it is necessary to plan to include what is required for the year. Hopefully this is reasonable in quantity, but at the same time has a breadth and balance of subjects. One suspects that there is always going to be more we would like to teach than we have time for. If the curriculum is not prescribed these decisions are made by the school or individual teachers.

When schools are large enough to have a two-form entry, long-term planning may become a team activity, with year group teachers meeting and planning together. Some schools feel that provision should be totally equable across the year and insist that medium-term planning is shared and delivered at the same time (within the same week). This has the advantage of sharing the workload of planning but can be a challenge on resource provision.

Further reading

The Standards site at www.standards.dfes.gov.uk gives more details.

TDA references

Q14, Q15, Q22, Q26, Q29.

Marking

We need to clearly establish why a piece of work is being marked. What purpose is your marking serving? Are the pupils clear about the purpose? As adults, we seek others to 'mark' draft versions of documents and letters that we write. We have developed our own checking strategies. There are sometimes opportunities to respond to top copy, i.e. the final version, as well. If the top copy is marked then there is an expectation to carry forward marking advice to the next appropriate situation. There are differences between the adult world and the school world, so maybe we should be creating stronger links between school and adult writing situations. For teachers the following questions might arise. Do children get an opportunity to draft work? Do they get the final draft marked or the top copy? How many top copies are expected and what is done with them? What status in the work system does the exercise book have? Do you write on 'top copy'?

In school, marking work is a traditional response to providing feedback, often brought about by large classes generating work faster than the teacher can monitor it. It can form a written record of a pupil's progress. It is also a measure of end product. Grading is a way of marking which allows comparison with classmates or against set criteria. Comments can be encouraging and constructive. Teachers often wonder if children act upon written advice and generally strategies are quite weak in ensuring pupils follow up the advice offered.

Consider also how useful the comments you make are going to be. What effect do comments such as, 'See me' and 'Satisfactory' have on pupils? Is 5/10 good, or did you expect everyone to gain 10/10? How does this mark look when parents examine the books on parents' evening? What sense will parents make of your comments? Sometimes the exercise books are the only evidence they see.

On draft work try to make comments which help children know what to do next. Make comments positive, perceptive and praiseworthy on final work. Try to mark with children present on some occasions and enter into a dialogue about the work. Try to have a quick turnaround on your marking as children are keen to have feedback as soon as possible. Allow time to address errors in a constructive way, maybe through discussion with peers or as a class. Encourage pupils to develop drafting and checking strategies.

You may wish to introduce an element of self-marking in some appropriate situations as this encourages children to seek their own feedback. It will be your responsibility to monitor these situations and get children to understand the significance of correct and incorrect answers. Competitive situations are difficult for children to deal with when self-marking.

Links

Active learning
Competition
Feedback
Formative assessment
Homework and out-of-class work
Independent learning
Parents and carers

Strategies

- Allow opportunities for pupils to respond to comments made by you (mark the final draft).
- Make comments encouraging with suggestions which pupils can act upon.
- Try to mark at least one piece of work during the week with the child.
- Respond to problems quickly by talking about them if possible.
- Mark and return work within 24–36 hours.
- Encourage self-editing and self-marking where appropriate.
- Encourage discussion about errors.
- Consider pupils producing work which they then use in class rather than have it marked.

Development

Marking is a practice which has been handed down almost as a tradition in teaching so maybe it is time to review the practice. A starting point for this might be to ask what purpose it serves in specific contexts. As a summative assessment response it has a clear function. As a formative assessment function there are situations where it may be better to provide alternative feedback of a constructive nature. If marking is used for formative purposes it needs to offer the pupil a way forward which they can act upon, such as, correcting a final draft rather than a top copy. Systems of self-assessment may be a strategy you choose to introduce alongside your own marking.

Black et al. (2004) have done extensive research on assessment for learning and their findings show that students who engage with formative feedback find it plays a significant part in their effective learning. Hayes (1999) offers good practical advice on marking and feedback and also quantifies the time it will take you. Decisions on marking will eventually affect what outputs you select and how much time you allow to address feedback during lessons. You also need to be clear about your own marking strategies as you may be required to justify them to parents. Consider what messages they are getting from their child, the child's homework, the child's work on parents' evenings and from the school's official policies and communications with them.

Further reading

Black, P., Harrison, C., Lee, C., Marshall, B. and Wiliam, D. (2004) *Assessment for Learning: Putting It into Practice*, Maidenhead: Open University Press.

Hayes, D. (1999) *Planning, Teaching and Class Management in Primary Schools*, London: David Fulton.

Sangster, M. and Overall, L. (2006) *Assessment: A practical guide for primary teachers*, London: Continuum.

TDA references

Q26, Q27, Q28.

Medium-term planning

This is the planning that takes place over a number of weeks. It draws upon the long-term planning or a syllabus. It is the stage where many teachers consider how they will teach an objective and what supporting activities they will require the children to carry out. They will also decide what resources they need to prepare or collect. Deciding on lessons which will generate good display material might be appropriate at this stage. Planning to include ICT could also be considered at the medium-term planning stage. It might be appropriate to differentiate at this stage. There is a balance of detail between the medium-term plans and the lesson plans depending on where you do your thinking about detail of delivery. It is possible that you opt to be well prepared in advance and then adjust your medium-term plans in the light of your lesson evaluations/pupils' performance.

Links

Differentiation
Lesson plan structure
Long-term planning
Resources

Strategies

- Draw upon long-term plans, curriculum documents and syllabi to establish the content of a block of work (e.g. half a term?).
- Consider objectives.
- Consider differentiation (and sub-objectives).
- Consider resources which need to be organized.
- Integrate the use of ICT.
- Plan for display work.
- Coordinate across subjects where possible (e.g. symmetry in maths, art and PE).

Development

Medium-term planning has similar issues to long-term planning strategies but some additional ones too. It is at this level that judgements are made about effective learning environments, teaching style and a variety of outputs from the children. Some of this is managing with what you have but there is some room to make choices and be inventive, to try out new approaches and instigate new systems of working with children.

Further reading

QCA schemes, examples of medium-term planning, can be found at www. teachernet.gov.uk

TDA references

Q14, Q15, Q22, Q26, Q29.

Misconceptions and remedies

Children often misunderstand or develop their own rules for deciding how something should be done. This is part of normal development. Learning things correctly saves children from developing misconceptions. Sometimes children's *ad hoc* rules work in specific situations, but are not correct in others. You need to be clear and correct in what you teach and observant of children's responses. On discovering a misconception it needs to be unlearned and a correct procedure/fact learned. This is harder than learning correctly in the first place! It might be necessary to go back many steps to resolve the problems.

In class, if the misconception arises with the majority of the class when you are teaching them, it is best to stop everyone and go over the point again. If you discover a common misconception when marking homework, it is worth taking a few minutes to address the problem with the whole class in the next lesson. There are various strategies that teachers use to get pupils to address corrections. One possibility is to let pupils discuss errors with each other, under your general supervision. As a pupil works during the lesson, it may be necessary to intervene because you can see misconceptions or errors developing. It is useful to question the pupil at this point about his/her thinking. Often, on reflection, he/she will see the error and, if not, you still get some indication of how he/she is working something out which will enable you to give appropriate advice.

Errors and misconceptions are seen by pupils as mistakes which are seen as a sign of failure. In actuality, they are often signposts on the frontiers of understanding, and as such, indicate where new learning needs to take place. Putting misconceptions right should be given a positive spin in the classroom rather than tucked away as, 'Five minutes to do your corrections before you go on to page twelve'.

Links

Active learning
Communicating clearly
Expectations about pupils' learning
Intellectual development
Lesson plan structure
Listening and responding to pupils

Strategies

- If a large number of pupils have not understood, stop the lesson and reiterate the point clearly.
- Allow time for pupils to discuss and correct errors.
- Plan time for discussion of mistakes and their causes.
- Question pupils about 'how' they have worked something out rather than launch into early explanation.
- When marking, certain mistakes can indicate misconceptions which you then need to check with the pupil.

Development

Teacher subject knowledge is an important factor in preventing misconceptions. Before teaching a topic try to research the pedagogic knowledge you require. Initially this can be a large part of your planning load but becomes easier as you call upon your previous experience. Sometimes we fall back on what we were taught ourselves and may be unaware that we too have misconceptions. For example, it is not uncommon to say in mathematics, 'When you multiply two numbers, the answer is bigger and when you divide two numbers the answer is smaller'. Consider the following:

$$\frac{1}{3} \times \frac{1}{3} = \frac{1}{9} \text{ (which is smaller)}$$

and then,

$$\frac{1}{3} \div \frac{1}{3} = \frac{3}{3} \text{ or } 1 \text{ (which is larger)}$$

This is a good example where the rule works with whole numbers but not when pupils start to extend the number system and deal with fractions. Try not to leave pupils without a way forward or without a solution to the problem when discussing misconceptions.

Further reading

Sangster, M. and Overall, L. (2006) *Assessment: A practical guide for primary teachers*, London: Continuum.

TDA reference

Q28.

Monitoring pupils' learning

See *Formative assessment.*

More able children

See *Able children.*

Motivation

Finding ways of interesting your pupils in the learning you want them to do is an excellent idea. Helping them to behave in acceptable ways so they can learn is also important. The learner's motivation is a key to this.

In school some children want to learn. Others are less keen! Some children expect to do well. Some are sure that they won't be able to do well. Some learners think they are successful because they are lucky, others think it is because they work hard, others because they are clever. This helps to explain why some children of similar ability achieve more than others.

Motivation is also to do with what individuals expect and want from the activity you've set. The child's reason for choosing, doing (performing) and keeping at (persisting) the tasks you set will vary.

Motivating pupils to learn is clearly a major preoccupation for teachers. You'll recognize that some pupils have *intrinsic motivation* that comes from internal sources such as curiosity, interest, pleasure, an innate need for mastery and growth. These pupils feel some sense of control over themselves. They are often concerned with the task rather than worrying about what others think about them. Others work better for rewards, known as *extrinsic motivation*, as it comes from an external source. These pupils want to succeed perhaps to avoid punishment, for a high mark or to please others. For most pupils, indeed most people, both systems operate at the same time.

Maslow (1970) suggested that there is a *hierarchy of needs* that has to be satisfied for people to do well. He suggests that lower order needs like having sufficient sleep and being loved have to be met before learning can take place. An example of this in school might be a child not learning because he/she is hungry, tired or frightened.

Links

Motivation is a key topic in these links:

Active learning
Competition
Differentiation
Discipline
Expectations about pupils' learning
Independent learning
Learning styles
Listening and responding to pupils
Purposeful working atmosphere
Research and its uses
Rewards
Target-setting

Strategies

- Your pupils need to feel valued. Aim for your classroom to be low on criticism and high on warmth (empathy). You and the pupils should celebrate achievement and limit blame.

- Emphasize personal judgement about personal capabilities to encourage pupils to think of their *successes as due to high ability* and attribute *lack of success to lack of effort*. A phrase like, 'You've worked hard' rewards effort; 'You're clever at that' confirms ability.
- Each child you teach needs to believe that he/she can succeed through effort. This means that you have to set tasks that enable success but require effort.

Development

In behaviourist theory the emphasis is on managing the learning situation with incentives and reinforcements built in. This standpoint suggests that the inner thoughts, feeling or psychological needs are not important, indeed they need not be considered for effective learning to occur. This is often the approach you'll use. Your use of rewards will include, for example, house points, or extra time on the computer, while punishments will include loss of privilege. Cognitive theorists, on the other hand, see motivation as a crucial element in learning. The strategies listed above start to deal with aspects of motivation. Motivation is to do with judgements a child makes about his/her ability to succeed at a task; self-evaluation is informed by what happened in the past, the models friends supply (think of peer pressure) and the feedback the child has had from others.

Further reading

Bigge, M. L. and Shermis, S. S. (1998) *Learning Theories for Teachers* (6th edn), New York: Addison Wesley Longman: An excellent introduction to the theoretical issues.

Maslow, A. (1970) *Motivation and Personality* (2nd edn), New York: Van Nostrand.

Overall, L. S. (2007) *Supporting Children's Learning*, London: Sage.

Pollard, A. with Collins, J., Maddock, M., Simco, N., Swaffield, S., Warin, J. and Warwick, P. (2005) *Reflective Teaching: Evidence-informed Professional Practice* (2nd edn), London: Continuum.

Whitebread, D. (ed.) (2000) *The Psychology of Teaching and Learning in the Primary School*, London: RoutledgeFalmer. Roland Chapman's chapter (6) on attribution theory is really helpful.

TDA reference

Q10.

Out-of-school learning opportunities

Children learn different things beyond the classroom and they really enjoy school visits. The reality is, they are educationally stimulating and memorable experiences. Visits, part of the day, a day or longer, can increase a child's competence and independence as a learner. They add an extra dimension to learning that is difficult to achieve in school.

To make the most, educationally, of a school visit you will need to prepare the children beforehand so that they can make sense of what they see. Usually visits are linked to the curriculum and therefore complement the work going on in the classroom.

During the visit you may ask children to look out for particular objects or events. If you have too much paperwork they will spend their time desperately trying to fill in the answers and miss much of what is going on. Think carefully about exactly what you want them to gain from the visit and then plan accordingly. For example, you might want Year 6 children to write about what it is like to live in an Iron Age round house, having visited the reconstruction. If there is a speaker it would be appropriate for the children to make notes during the talk. You may then ask them for a list of adjectival phrases while they observe the surroundings and take in the atmosphere.

On returning to school you should allow time for follow-up work. This work could vary in form, from drama to displays, booklets to creative writing or scientific experiment.

When planning the visit account for: all the costs, including transport; adult supervision; the schedule; informing parents and carers; what you want and do not want children to bring (in writing); necessary permission (from headteacher, governors, parents and carers, local authority).

The benefits of taking children on visits greatly outweigh the risks. You will be expected to assess the hazards and make sure that children are going to be reasonably safe. You are advised to read the link on *Safety* which summarizes some of the actions you should take. There will be specific considerations about hazards and risks for particular out-of-school learning.

As far as you can you will want to ensure that all children can have the opportunity to go. This will mean that the visit is suitable and accessible to all. Extra expense is a huge burden for some parents. Some children have special needs, medical conditions, cultural or religious requirements that need to be accounted for in setting up the activity. Sometimes you will need to make a hard decision to deny a pupil whose behaviour is likely to be unreliable, the chance to accompany the class. Where children are not able to go, you need to ensure that this aspect of the curriculum is provided in other ways.

Links

Discipline
Expectations about pupils' learning
Foundation stage

Long-term planning
Medium-term planning
Primary National Strategy
Safety

Strategies

All these factors need to be considered:

- Include visits in long- and medium-term planning.
- Build in appropriate preparation and follow-up work.
- Get permission from necessary authorities, including parents and carers.
- Book visit, guides, speakers and transport.
- Organize adult supervision and check health and safety factors including completion of risk assessment.
- Inform parents and carers, and pupils, of schedule and food, money and clothing requirements.
- Have a great day.

Further reading

www.baalpe.org The British Association of Advisers & Lecturers in PE has definitive information in Safe Practice in Physical Education. This is an excellent starting place for making out-of-school activities safe and enjoyable. See their website for the details.

www.teachernet.gov.uk/wholeschool/healthandsafety/visits is essential reading for planning safe visits.

TDA references

Q24, Q30.

Pace

The right pace is achieved when you have the pupils' attention, as learning is most likely to take place when they are engaged. Getting the pace of a lesson right is challenging because children learn at different rates. In oral sessions you will be trying to work at a speed which engages your more able children, but also allows the rest of the class to understand, including those who learn more slowly. This can be thought of as communicating at several levels through the language you use, the content of the work and the general class and individual questions you ask.

If your explanations are too long or you ask too many questions which require long answers, you risk lowering the overall pace. As the pace slows, some children stop paying attention and possibly begin to misbehave. If the pace is too fast, some children fail to comprehend the teaching points and are unable to do follow-up tasks. In either example, learning does not take place.

Poor behaviour can lead to the teacher engaging in one-to-one discipline talks which further slows the pace of the lesson and other pupils' behaviour can begin to deteriorate. Deal quickly with behaviour problems or sort them out at the end of the oral session. Better still, try and anticipate them and have strategies to forestall them. (For example, sit the children who find concentration a problem near you in carpet sessions.)

When children are doing tasks, pace is important too. It is useful to give them completion times and targets to remind them of this during the task period. For example, 'You should have answered at least three questions by now' and 'You have ten minutes left, so begin to check your work'. Pupils need to learn to stay on task so make this a clear expectation. Differentiation is important because this allows the task to be manageable.

Links

Differentiation
Discipline
Motivation
Questioning

Strategies

- Raise the pace if children are restless. Lower the pace if you want to give the pupils time to think.
- Extend or shorten oral sessions depending on whether the pupils are engaged in the work.
- Use a mixture of questions that elicit long and short answers.
- Differentiate questions and content to include the range of ability of the class in oral sessions and group tasks.
- Decide when it is time to move on (as pupils begin to disengage).
- Convey expectations about completion of work and time available.
- Check through the lesson that you are maintaining your timing (only change this if you can justify it to yourself).
- Avoid lengthy one-to-ones about off-task behaviour in whole-class situation. (anticipate, then deal with them quickly or later).

Development

The Hay McBer report (2000: 1.2.9) states, 'Effective teachers achieve the management of the class by having a clear structure for each lesson, making full use of planned time, using a brisk pace and allocating his/her time fairly amongst pupils'. Getting the pace right by being sensitive to how the children are responding and being well organized will go a long way to ensuring the children are on task for a high percentage of your lesson.

Kounin (1970) observed teachers communicating with their classes and found four types of action that teachers took which disrupted the flow of their lessons. He described these as dangles, flip flops, overdwelling and fragmentation.

- The dangles left the delivery unfinished.
- The flip flop was a change of subject mid-sentence.
- The overdwelling was spending too long on a topic already grasped by the pupils.
- The fragmentation was splitting up the work into so many small steps that the pupils lost the purpose of the lesson.

The general impetus is to increase the pace to ensure pupils' attention and reasonable behaviour. It is worth considering whether the pace matches the task. It would be quite easy for pupils to abdicate from higher order thinking when the teacher moves on too quickly and does not allow enough time to work something out.

Further reading

Hay McBer (2000) *Research into Teacher Effectiveness: A Model of Teacher Effectiveness*, London: DfEE (www.dfes.gov.uk/teachingreforms/leadership/mcber).
Kounin, J. (1970) *Discipline and Group Management in the Classroom*, New York: Holt Reinhart and Winston.
Sangster, M. and Overall, L. (2006) *Assessment: A practical guide for primary teachers*, London: Continuum.

TDA reference

Q25(c, d).

Parents and carers

Who are parents?

This depends on the circumstances. The child's natural parents, either or both mother and father, may not always be the person/people with responsibility. Step-parents, relatives, co-habitees of step-parents and relatives, adoptive parents may all take on parental responsibility. In the UK, foster carers and people employed by local authorities to care for children subject to residence orders or care orders are not treated in the same way by Education Acts, but in practical terms will often be treated by school authorities as taking parental responsibility.

The people who care for the pupils in your class have rights and responsibilities. Your respect for them is central to establishing and maintaining a working relationship. See the entry on *Communication with parents and carers* for further information and reading.

What is parental responsibility?

These are all the rights, duties, powers and responsibilities which a parent of a child has by law. For example, in the UK, it is a parental responsibility to ensure that school-aged children attend school.

What is parenting style?

The way that children are dealt with at home will make a difference to their response to teachers and peers. Some parents and carers are very strict and controlling: they adopt an authoritarian style. This may mean that children have too little freedom to develop. Some give children opportunities to make mistakes and support their development in many ways: this authoritative style enables development. Others give in to the child's whim: an indulgent style may mean that the child has no boundaries within which to develop. Some seem not to care to deal with their child's development: an uninvolved style may mean that the child has no boundaries and little home support. You will draw your own conclusions about the influence of parenting style on the way the children you teach learn and behave.

Links

Communication with parents and carers
Relationships with pupils

Further reading

Both these sites are directed at parents and carers, they are included because they give some insight into the UK government's understanding about the role of teachers (and other professionals):

www.everychildmatters.gov.uk/parents

www.parentscentre.gov.uk

TDA references

Q4, Q5.

Personalized learning

See *Active learning, Independent learning.*

Physical development

Factors such as cultural practices, nutrition and experiences all influence physical growth and development. Heredity is likely to determine eventual height and physical appearance. This helps to account for the considerable physical differences you'll see between children of the same age.

Human growth is comparatively slow. It is not until between a year and 14 months that most children can walk unaided. Physical development is at its most rapid in infancy, children get taller and stronger more rapidly between 0–five years. Growth slows from about age six until the onset of puberty. Until puberty, differences in height, weight and muscle mass between girls and boys are slight, for example, both sexes can be expected to have a similar ability to run and jump.

The onset of puberty brings changes in the sexual characteristics. It is worth knowing about the changes that occur, as the psychological effects are considerable for some adolescents. Parents and carers and pupils are often surprisingly uninformed about puberty. With the consent of the parents and carers, as a teacher you are often well placed to give accurate information to your children. There will be some children in primary school who start to go through these changes. Physical development at this stage is complex. There are changes in the reproductive system, in the cardiovascular system and the lungs, with an affect on the respiration system and the size and strength of many muscles in the body. Often there is a 'growth spurt'. The variation between the onset of puberty and the rate of growth between individuals is considerable. In secondary school there are students of the same age who are young men and women, working alongside others who are still children. Although this is perfectly normal it can be a source of considerable anxiety both to adolescents and their parents and carers. The growth spurt may start as young as nine for some boys but may not happen until 15. Girls may start younger, as young as seven or eight, but may not until they are 12, 13 or 14. The average, though, for boys is around 12 and between 10–11 for girls.

Links

Emotional development
Intellectual development
Linguistic development
Research and its uses
Social development

Further reading

Meece, J. L. (1997) *Child and Adolescent Development for Educators*, New York: McGraw Hill.

Oates, J. (ed.) (1994) *The Foundations of Child Development*, Milton Keynes: Open University and Blackwells.
Ken Richardson's Chapter 6 'Interactions in Development' is an interesting introduction to some of the complexities in this area.

TDA reference

Q18.

Play and structured learning

The role of play in human development is much debated. It may be a need which continues through life but takes different forms as we grow older. Within the education system play is seen as a need for young children and in most curricula there is an expectation that children will have opportunities to play. Play situations can range from child-controlled play, through varying degrees of teacher-controlled situations.

Teachers set up various types of play situations. Firstly there is completely free play where children choose what they are going to do and what equipment/toys they are going to use. This is akin to children's experience in the early years at home and in play school. In the primary school this can still be seen in Reception classes and of course, all the way through the school at break-times. In the classroom/nursery, a common practice is for the teacher to set out equipment which is relevant to a theme/objective which is being promoted and there may even be an indication of who is to use the equipment, but no task is set. An example of this further up the primary school can be seen when teachers and teaching assistants prepare interactive displays. Open task situations such as this can be followed up by the teacher joining a group and intervening with questions and related teaching points. The third situation is when the teacher sets a task with the selected equipment.

Finally, the teacher may initiate and control the whole task. (Setting the task without selecting the equipment moves us into the territory of problem solving; 'What shall I use to solve this task?') As you can see, through this range there is a move towards structured learning similar to that found in classes of older children. The expectation to attend and respond to the teachers' agenda is gradually developed. This does not mean that free play situations should be eliminated.

Links

Creativity
Displays
Emotional development
Foundation stage
Intellectual development
Intervention
Primary National Strategy
Problem solving
Resources
Social development

Strategies

- Decide whether the situation is going to be entirely free, or if equipment and/or tasks are going to be set.
- How much teacher intervention is planned? Is it at the beginning or towards the end of the task?

Development

One cannot mention young children and play without paying due respect to the philosophies of educational giants such as Montessori, Steiner and Isaacs, whose theoretical standpoints are highly influential in nursery education. Collecting empirical evidence on the exact role of play in learning has proved difficult, partly because the word encompasses many different types of activity and partly because researchers look for different outcomes. A useful account of theory, past research and research with teachers of five year olds can be found in *Teaching Through Play* (Bennett et al., 1997). Play may have links with assimilation of learning and creativity but in education systems where immediate learning is expected on prescribed objectives, play can come under pressure for not delivering tangible results. Play must be considered within the early years' curriculum and teachers should decide on its value and create a range of opportunities from free play through to structured tasks.

An issue to consider is whether primary classrooms are too structured. Is there a danger that structure stifles spontaneity, decision making and creativity? With more prescribed curricula it is tempting to justify rigorous target-setting for each lesson so that children progress through the curriculum at a rapid rate.

Further reading

Bennett, N., Wood, L. and Rogers, S. (1997) *Teaching Through Play*, Buckingham: Open University Press.
See *The Standards Site* (www.standard.dfes.gov.uk) for the *Framework for Early Years Foundation Stage*, which gives further information.

TDA references

Q3(a), Q10, Q15.

Primary National Strategy

On 20 May 2003 the British government published *Excellence and Enjoyment – A Strategy for Primary Schools* in which it laid out its vision for the future of primary school education. Its aims were stated as follows:

The key to making this vision a reality lies in:

- Empowering primary schools to take control of their curriculum, and to be more innovative and to develop their own character.
- Schools setting their own targets for levels 4 and 5 at key stage 2, based on challenging but realistic targets for the progress of each child in the school, with LEA targets being set afterwards.
- Trialling a new approach of supported teacher assessment at KS1, where tests underpin teacher assessment rather than being reported separately.
- Encouraging schools to network together and learning from others in sharing and developing good practice. Partnership with parents, which is vital in helping children to do as well as they can, and making wider links with the community.
- Government acting more and more as an enabler with schools increasingly in control of the support they get to:
  1. strengthen leadership, particularly leadership of teaching, and professional development to help teachers embed the principles of effective teaching and learning both in literacy and numeracy and across the curriculum

2. help schools design broad and rich curricula which make the most of links between different areas and provide opportunities for children to have a wide range of learning experiences.

(www.standards.dfes.gov.uk/primary/about (accessed 9/06))

This is an attempt to bring together the various initiatives which have been introduced into primary schools since 1997. During this time there has been a growing awareness of the need to see children in the context of their whole lives (*Every Child Matters*) and not have schools as isolated institutions, nor have subject study as separate entities. The Primary National Strategy encourages teachers to introduce a more creative curriculum, have a greater cross-curricular approach but at the same time maintain the progress made in literacy and numeracy.

Links

Creativity
Foundation stage
Primary National Strategy

Further reading

Excellence and Enjoyment at www.standards.dfes.gov.uk/primary/publications/literacy/63553
Literacy at www.standards.dfes.gov.uk/primary/literacy
Numeracy at www.standards.dfes.gov.uk/primary/mathematics
The National Curriculum: www.curriculumonline.gov.uk/Default.htm
The Primary Strategy at www.standards.dfes.gov.uk/primary/about/

TDA reference

Q3(a).

Problem solving

Life is full of problems that need to be solved, therefore this is a process which needs to be present in education. Much has been written about the skills and processes involved in problem solving in different subjects. Whether you see it as a way into new work or as an opportunity to apply acquired knowledge, it is an essential life skill and a rationale for gaining new skills and knowledge (using what you learn).

Sometimes when teachers provide children with problems and investigations and the children fail to get started or do not come up with a solution. As in real life, no one can immediately solve all problems. Often time is needed to try different strategies or make a useful mental link or acquire new relevant knowledge. What children do need is knowledge of the strategies or processes which can be used to try and solve problems. These need to be overtly taught just like the rest of the curriculum. Getting started, sorting the data, seeking patterns, linking to what you know, trying out a theory, testing a theory, etc. are all ways of working which we have to help children understand and use.

Links

Active learning
Explaining
Group work
Independent learning
Intervention
Listening and responding to pupils
Skills and strategies
Thinking skills

Strategies

- Include problem solving in medium-term planning in suitable subjects.
- Help children with processes by teaching and discussing them (as lesson objectives?).
- Do 'whole class' problem solving to start with to demonstrate the thinking processes they need to use.
- Use problem solving to consolidate work and to assess whether children have a working knowledge of a piece of learning.
- Or, use a problem to introduce a topic and engage interest.
- Develop a range of verbal 'prompts' to help children think about their work when they are stuck (which can be in the form of a set of questions).
- Reassure pupils that work often leads to 'dead ends' and they need to go back and pick up a new thread.

Development

You can set problems that have a single step and one solution such as, 'What two paints do you mix to create orange?' Other problems have many steps before you arrive at the solution. A common error that children make is to find a solution but not check back to see if it answers the original question. For example, in a question which asks for the number of minibuses needed to transport a class of 39 children to the swimming pool when each bus holds 12 children, a child answers, 'You need 3.25 minibuses'. A further step in rounding up needs to be taken to give a realistic answer of four. A further set of problems are those that are open ended. Sometimes these open-ended problems are known as investigations. They also offer the opportunity for children to make decisions and pose questions. There are opportunities within them to decide which lines of enquiry you will pursue. Children may have different solutions and even more questions in this type of enquiry. All these forms of work require children to develop a process of tackling problems which brings together use of their prior knowledge and generic strategies for what to do next. Fisher (1987) writes about the processes primary school children employ in problem solving. His strategies are in the form of a series of child-friendly questions.

Further reading

Burton, L. (1984) *Thinking Things Through*, Oxford: Blackwell.

Fisher, R. (1987) *Problem Solving in the Primary School*, Oxford: Blackwell.

TDA reference

Q25.

Purposeful working atmosphere

It is important to have a purposeful working atmosphere because it is in this environment that learning is most likely to take place. There is also the implication that children will be engaged in work they see as meaningful and are therefore motivated to do. Many factors come together to create this kind of environment. A purposeful working atmosphere is often observed in classrooms where the teachers believe children should be independent learners; it appears that this is more likely to be achieved if the children see the work as their work, rather than something that is totally imposed by the teacher. Others would argue that this is not true; it is purely a matter of clarity of purpose and good organization that creates a purposeful working atmosphere.

Whichever view you hold, to move towards achieving a purposeful working atmosphere it is important that all the children understand what they are working towards and that the work is at a level in which they can engage and contribute. This will assist in helping them to stay on task. It is the teacher's responsibility to motivate the children to complete the task and complete it well. The teacher must make it clear what standard of work, behaviour and style of working they expect in their classroom. This is often done quite overtly when the teacher first begins to work with the class and is gently reinforced over a period of time.

Links

Communication about learning
Discipline
Equal opportunities
Expectations about pupils' learning
Listening and responding to pupils
Motivation
Relationships with pupils
Target-setting

Strategies

- Clear expectations of how the children are going to go about the work.
- Well-differentiated work (lesson planning and formative assessment).
- Attainable and clearly stated objectives, shared with the children.
- Generate an enthusiasm in the children to do the work (motivation).
- Well-organized resources.
- Encourage children to take responsibility through decision making about their own work.

Development

Underpinning a purposeful working environment will be a well-established relationship between the teacher and the pupils. The pupils should understand that the teacher is interested in what they are doing and they should know the rules of conduct and work procedures in the class. In return, the teacher provides a stimulating environment, fairness of action and a genuine interest in the work and welfare of his/her pupils.

Physically, the classroom should be clean, tidy and warm, with stimulating display material on the walls and shelves. Children will want to be there. They may even have a sense of ownership and contribute by being monitors/helpers.

The teacher will also ensure that the work environment is non-threatening. It will be a place where children feel that they are able to contribute, even if it is only a tentative suggestion. There will be no fear that they are going to be ridiculed by their peers or rejected by the teacher.

TDA reference

Q30.

Questioning

There are several different types of questioning which elicit different forms of response from pupils. The most common form of questioning observed in the classroom is: teacher asks question, pupil gives short response, teacher gives a short response indicating whether he/she approves of the answer, or thinks it is wrong. This closed questioning is designed to get a simple, often anticipated response, for example, 'What is the capital of France?' or, 'What is 9 x 7?'

Open questions are those where a pupil might offer any one of a range of answers or explanations. For example, 'How could you work that out?' or, 'What do you think happens next in the story?' Open questions promote children's articulation of their thinking.

Children are very good at working out whether they have given a successful answer. They read the teacher's body language and interpret the teacher's responses. For example, if a teacher frowns slightly or says, 'Are you sure?', they will assume they have given a wrong answer and will often offer an alternative response. However, 'Are you sure?' might be the teacher being genuinely interested, asking the pupil to justify their response. Children, however, quickly get used to the pattern of your questioning.

When children are struggling, sometimes it is a better strategy to question what they have done so far or suggest a way forward. These are 'prompt' questions and help children to articulate their thinking. Often this allows a child to see a way forward for themselves. As you work with your pupils you should increasingly expect them to justify their responses.

Links

Active learning
Communication about learning
Demonstration by the teacher
Explaining

Feedback
Independent learning
Instruction
Intervention
Listening and responding to pupils
Pace
Thinking skills
Whole-class teaching

Strategies

- Use a range of question types.
- When you want to increase the pace of an oral session use closed questions.
- When you want to explore children's thinking and encourage their explanations, use more open questions.
- To promote consolidation of understanding ask children to talk about what they have done.
- If a child is stuck, use a 'prompt' question.
- Experiment with the balance between your information giving and your questioning.
- Increase the level of demand for explanations and justification as appropriate to an individual's progress.

Development

Perrot (1996) offers an analysis of questioning in whole-class oral situations and offers strategies for use of different types of questioning, including higher order questions which are aimed at eliciting responses which require pupils to think. Such questions might require them to analyse information, offer informed opinion or make new links between known facts.

Hayes (1999) gives a useful summary of the use of questioning by the teacher and then moves on to the importance of pupils developing their own questioning skills. It is very much the teacher's responsibility to create a classroom environment where it is alright to ask questions. It is very easy to misuse questions about work to discipline poor behaviour or inattentiveness (Galton, 1996). This leads to a reluctance to answer academic questions, so make behaviour questions/statements clearly about behaviour only.

Black et al. (2004) in their research with secondary school students identified good questioning by the teacher and the pupils as contributing to increased engagement in thinking by pupils which in turn leads to an increase in understanding. Clarke (2001) considers carefully how pupils in primary schools respond to questioning. They pick up cues from the teacher's tone and body language and also gauge how peers will react to their responses. This sensitivity to the opinion of others increases as pupils enter secondary education. Question and response carries many social nuances but can be one of the most powerful tools for learning. For a more detailed discussion on questioning refer to Sangster and Overall (2006).

Further reading

Black, P., Harrison, C., Lee, C., Marshall, B. and Wiliam, D. (2004) *Assessment for Learning: Putting It into Practice*, Maidenhead: Open University Press.

Brown, G. and Wragg, E. (1993) *Questioning*, London: Routledge.

Clarke, S. (2001) *Unlocking Formative Assessment*, London: Hodder and Stoughton.

Galton, M. (1996) 'Ambiguity in learning', in Pollard, A. (ed.) *Readings for Reflective Teaching in the Primary School*, London: Continuum.

Hayes, D. (1999) *Planning Teaching and Class Management in Primary Schools*, London: David Fulton.

Perrot, E. (1996) 'Using questions in classroom discussions', in Pollard, A. (ed.) *Readings for Reflective Teaching in the Primary School*, London: Continuum.

Sangster, M. and Overall, L. (2006) *Assessment: A Practical Guide for Primary Teachers*, London: Continuum. Chapter 9 is devoted to 'questioning'.

TDA reference

Q25(c).

Recording individual progress

When considering what you are going to record, always be clear about the purpose, as this will help you identify what is most useful to collect evidence about (assessment criteria).

Recording individual progress happens at various levels and for different purposes. In the classroom you will probably wish to keep detailed 'informal notes' about children meeting specific objectives or having difficulty. This is done to enable you to keep track of how each child is progressing. These 'notes' will feed into your lesson planning and could be used to inform a more official record.

At the next level there will be particular information which needs to be passed on to others such as the SENCO (Special Educational Needs Co-ordinator), the next teacher, parents and carers, school records or the next school. Schools often decide on the nature of the information they wish to send or receive.

A third level is official and legal. There are requirements to report on individual progress to parents and local authorities (LAs). In England there are legal requirements for information on annual reports to parents and teacher assessment within the Key Stage assessment procedures (see Summative assessment).

Links

Formative assessment
Marking
Parents and carers
Special educational needs
Summative assessment
Target-setting

Strategies

- Before teaching, decide what assessment system you will run.
- Before teaching, devise appropriate recording formats.
- Choose manageable assessment criteria and ones that will inform you about children's understanding.
- Check what information needs to be collected over the long term (half-term, term, year). Devise a strategy to ensure you can acquire this evidence.
- Build into your planning a strategy to deal with the findings of your assessments (i.e. when will you deal with individuals who do not understand this work; day-to-day, week-to-week, medium term?).

Development

For teachers who spend a complete year with the children in their classes, recording is more likely to be done in the medium term. These teachers have a wealth of experience against which to measure those who lie outside the normal range of progress. As a student teacher, recording serves several purposes. One purpose is to track individuals and inform the teacher of their progress at the end of the practice. Another is to ensure you develop assessment procedures as part of the teaching cycle. Your recording will provide evidence for you and your mentor of how consistent you are in collecting information about individuals and how you use that information. One purpose of teaching practice is that it is the place where you will to try out a variety of assessment and recording methods, which will then be required when you get your own class to teach.

Further reading

Sangster, M. and Overall, L. (2006) *Assessment: A practical guide for primary teachers*, London: Continuum.

TDA references

Q27, Q28.

Relationships with pupils

The way you work with your pupils, what you say to them, how you treat them and the respect you show them, helps to build your reputation. If you think back to your own school days, you'll recall the teachers you liked and those you disliked. You will be with the children in your class every school day for a whole year. As well as the children expecting you to teach them, they will expect other things from you. Beyond achievement in their work, they would like you to be approachable, take an interest in them and know about them as people. Particularly for the younger children, you are a cross between a parent and carers and a representation of authority. They will value firmness but will appreciate approachability.

Your personal code of conduct will be based on your understanding of ethical principles, legal requirements, contract of employment, the job, and the role and expectations that other colleagues, parents and carers and the community beyond the school have. There are some things that are never acceptable, for example, a sexual liaison with someone you teach, advocating illegal acts and promoting a particular political party. You should be cautious about any meetings with any pupil on a one-to-one basis; for example, 'Come in on Saturday morning to help me finish this project'. Always make sure that several children or other adults are around. It would be naïve not to safeguard your professional reputation.

Links

Bullying
Child protection
Emotional development
Equal opportunities
Inclusion
Listening and responding to pupils
Motivation
Purposeful working atmosphere
Social development
Teachers' employment and conditions
Values and ethos

Strategies

Recognize that children have expectations about you. All you have to do is teach well and treat them fairly. If their past experience of teachers was poor, your task initially will be much harder. Take account of learners' feelings and emotions. What are their anxieties? How motivated are they?

- Share your excitement and enthusiasm for learning.
- Respect your pupils by preparing to meet their different needs. Accept their standards, either high or low, as a starting place for better things.
- Praise effort, celebrate achievement on an individual basis.
- Set able pupils higher targets and encourage discussion.
- Be aware of your own views about race, gender, class and special needs. Make sure that you treat pupils fairly by sharing out your time evenly.
- Be approachable, teaching is a two-way process; promote genuine discussion.
- Be yourself, teaching does use acting skills but pupils very soon know more about you than you often know yourself.
- Avoid remarks that may be perceived as negative, be careful that your jokes are not at someone else's expense.

Development

Sometimes the way we are required to deal with pupils conflicts with our personal set of values. For example, you may not care about whether a pupil is in school uniform or not, but in your school it is the rule, so you're expected to enforce the school dress code. This is where you need to uphold professional standards. If there is a mismatch between your views and school policy you must seek to make your case at policy level, not at pupil level.

Further reading

Cowley, S. (2003) *How to Survive your First Year in Teaching*, London: Continuum.

Pollard, A. with Collins, J., Maddock, M., Simco, N., Swaffield, S., Warin, J. and Warwick, P. (2005) *Reflective Teaching: Evidence-informed Professional Practice* (2nd edn), London: Continuum. Chapter 6 deals comprehensively with the issues.

Thody, A., Gray, B. and Bowden, D. (2000) *The Teacher's Survival Guide*, London: Continuum.

TDA references

Q1, Q4, Q27, Q28.

Research and its uses

'What research questions should I be asking?' 'What's worth spending precious time on?' Research questions can arise from what you do in your teaching, through questioning your own knowledge about the content of your subject. You will want to find out why some of your teaching is more effective, some less so, and more about the ways in which children learn best. In your school, you might ask, 'What are the best solutions to the challenges here?' Beyond the school you need to know about issues so that you can question these. Furthermore, it is a proper and a legitimate use of your time. In England research is a Teacher and Development Agency (TDA) Standard. It is also part of the General Teaching Council's professional code. For your own professionalism it is important for you to be a learner, risk taker and an explorer, after all, this is what we ask children to do. Research for teachers has several aspects: it supports subject knowledge, how we teach and also addresses wider issues.

Knowledge about the subjects you teach needs to be kept up-to-date. From time to time curriculum development means that you will need to learn something new. You need to know what children may find hard to learn so that you can pay extra attention to making this as easy as possible for them. To do this you'll research subjects thoroughly; you'll make sure that what you are teaching is accurate.

As a teacher you have expectations about the children in your class. You will be thinking all the time of ways that you can make the concepts and knowledge they need really interesting and easy for them to learn. You will want to know that the way you teach is as effective as possible and your reflections about the relationships between teaching and learning will lead you into doing research on the subject, in order to be more knowledgeable about it. You will want children to look forward to your lessons, even when the ideas are difficult. At first you will plan some of your teaching following ideas that work for other teachers. With experience your repertoire of teaching approaches will expand. The research question is, 'What works for me?' You will want to put yourself in a strong position to argue for your approach. You will be basing your teaching on something other than a hunch, or 'it works because it works'. Your research will take the form of assessing the effectiveness of your actions through the evidence you collect from learning taking place in your own classroom.

Keeping yourself informed about issues beyond the classroom means that you will know what policies are likely to impact on your work. An international perspective is important as well. Reading the education press and professional journals alerts you to the world beyond the classroom. This will often inform your reflection on your own practice. Your information will be used in discussions with colleagues.

Links

Active learning
Independent learning
Teachers' employment and conditions

Strategies

- Question your own ways of knowing through reading, networking and keeping up-to-date on issues.
- Read the research:
  i   read critically and find alternative views to make the most of research;
  ii survey the literature by reading the summaries rather than whole articles;
  iii use databases such as British Educational Index (BEI) and Educational Resources Information Centre (ERIC) to locate the areas that interest you;
  iv carry out searches for particular information through search engines that are appropriate for your task, be aware that the internet has both splendidly authoritative sources and the most awful rubbish available on it, with all shades in between.
- Network with others who are interested in similar areas through local professional groups, local university contacts and national and international associations.
- In the UK use the websites of official bodies such as the TDA, Department for Education and Skills (DfES), Office for Standards in Education (Ofsted), Qualifications and Curriculum Agency (QCA) and British Educational Communications and Technology Agency (BECTa) to identify the issues that they think important. Note: these bodies are policy making so the research they support and commission is often related to a particular view.
- Use university and teacher centre librarians to obtain access to the best research.
- Seek sponsorship for classroom enquiry and continuing professional development (e.g. DfES, TDA, and other organizations can offer opportunities for funding).

Development

As you teach you will be thinking about the research you have read and making connections with your work. You may well start to develop an interest in a particular aspect of teaching. At that point you will want to ask your own research questions. When you are ready to carry out some research of your own, training and support is offered by universities. You may be able to fund this through your school's staff development fund, or through grants made for this purpose from a variety of sources. Teachers who choose to research practice often find it very tough going but they also admit that the challenge was worthwhile and invigorating.

Further reading

Banks, F. and Shelton Mayes, A. (eds) (2001) *Early Professional Development for Teachers*, London: Open University/David Fulton. Section 3 has an interesting selection of articles about research.

Pring, R. (2000) *Philosophy of Education Research*, London: Continuum.

www.becta.org.uk

www.DfES.uk.gov

www.ofsted.uk.gov

www.qca.org.uk

www.teachernet.uk.gov

TDA references

Q7, Q8, Q9.

Resources

Good resources can provide a stimulating start to a lesson as well as offering useful visual images (a picture is worth a thousand words?). Well-resourced practical work enhances the learning environment because children are able to work in a physical as well as mental medium.

There are two kinds of resources; those that are readily available in your classroom from day to day, and those you have to acquire or make. This second group need to be considered when you do your medium-term planning to allow you time to assemble them. The second group of resources might include, posters, a collection of objects, a set of demonstration number cards, a collection of artefacts from a historical period or books and videos for a particular topic.

When you are considering the resources you are going to use, take into account social, cultural and gender implications and ensure you provide a fair curriculum for your children. Schools are not wealthy and sometimes resources such as books can be quite old. Check that the textbooks you use are appropriate for children growing up in this day and age. It is part of your role as a teacher to ensure you monitor the resources available to children in your classroom.

Links

Culture
Differentiation

Equal opportunities
Formative assessment
Purposeful working atmosphere
Social development

Strategies

- Plan at medium-term level for resources you need to make or acquire.
- Try and find resources that illustrate well the teaching points.
- Create a visually stimulating environment (interactive too).
- Use a variety of resources to capture attention.
- Use resources to bring the outside world into the classroom (art, pictures of other countries, posters with messages about the environment, etc.).
- Update and check your resources are appropriate for modern society.

Development

Over a century ago when education for very young children was new territory, Froebel devised a series of educational toys which, through play, would promote children's understanding of logical and mathematical relationships. This is early evidence of the recognition that resources can aid children's learning. Nowadays in primary schools there are a wide range of resources on offer to support children's learning. Unfortunately, schools never seem to have quite enough money to buy all the resources they would like. Many teachers and teaching assistants are ingenious at making their own resources. These are often the most effective too because the teacher knows what is appropriate for his or her children and what is going to be effective in illustrating what he or she wants to teach. Good ideas for teaching are now abundant on websites as well as in books. When planning to use resources, make sure they are prepared so time is not wasted in lessons. When planning to use resources select those which support the learning that you expect to take place. Occasionally resources can be used as an open-ended stimulus. Sometimes children bring things into the classroom which can be opportunities for spontaneous learning.

When developing independent learning there will be times when you expect children to make decisions about what resources they think are going to help them carry out a task. How are your resources organized? Are they accessible to the children? Do they need to ask you for everything or are certain things openly available? How do you organize for resources to be kept tidy? Is tidiness an expectation of every individual or do you have monitors? If you have monitors does this mean children can leave things out because they know others will 'clear up'? Think through the implications of your organization.

Further reading

An example of a teacher resource site is the BBC Schools resources which can be found at
www.teacherxpress.com/f.php?gid=17&id=4

National Curriculum at www.curriculumonline.gov.uk

Teacher training resource bank (ttrb) at www.ttrb.ac.uk is a site which links you to many quality teacher training resources through a system similar to Google. It provides reference for easy to return to sites. It includes links to government documents and Teachers' TV.

Teachers' TV www.teachers.tv

TDA reference

Q25(a).

Rewards

Do not undervalue the power of positive comment. As human beings we respond to praise and encouragement. The need to be 'overt' with young children sometimes makes this feel excessive but, as long as the pupil's action is worthy of praise, then be unstinting with it. Praise does wonders for pupils' confidence and motivation. It is a challenge in any classroom to avoid being negative. When only positive comments are heard aloud it has the effect of creating a positive classroom environment where children are happy to work. If you have to tell someone off, it is appropriate to speak to them quietly on a one-to-one basis and always leave them with a way forward.

Rewards can be verbal and non-verbal, such as a smile or placing good work on display, or asking them to tell the rest of the class about their work in the plenary.

Rewards can also be more tangible. They can be part of a behaviourist approach to learning. Good behaviour and work is reinforced by rewards (points, sweets, praise, sharing work with a wider audience, etc.). Rewards can be used by the teacher as an overt indicator of quality work. Be sure to reward quality work rather than a large quantity of mediocre work.

Links

Competition
Discipline
Motivation

Strategies

- Try to make sure all whole-class comments are either positive or instructional.
- Deal with poor work/behaviour on a one-to-one basis.
- Use rewards in appropriate situations such as:
  - good behaviour
  - good effort
  - a small step of improved performance
  - quality work.
- Be fair in offers of rewards.
- Do not withdraw awards already given.
- Be explicit in your praise, e.g. 'I liked the way you asked Simon to let you use his paint brush', 'You've got seven of those sums done, the answers are correct, that's good work'.

Development

Some schools use powerful reward systems to instigate new behaviour and work patterns. One such system is called, 'Smarties in the Jar', with the children banking points through the week for good behaviour and work, then the best group and individuals are rewarded with treats, such as extra break-time. Cumulative good responses from a class might be rewarded with a school visit. This is a strong, behaviourist strategy to encourage change, which utilizes the desire for reward and willingness to compete.

Behaviourist research (Skinner, 1974) indicated that removal of rewards does not eliminate poor behaviour. Skinner believed that rewards need to be frequently reinforced to establish good behaviour.

Further reading

Skinner, B. (1974) *About Behaviourism*, London: Cape.
Overall, L. S. (2007) *Supporting Children's Learning*, London: Sage.

TDA references

Q25, Q26.

Safety

Everyone who works in school has a *duty of care* to keep children safe. For teachers the duty of care implies more than acting as a 'good and careful parent'. In the UK and many other countries, teachers have a statutory obligation to assess risks in all types of situations. Risk assessments involving physical safety are likely to be high on most schools' agendas. You will see teachers taking care over how pupils are trained to behave when faced with physical danger, however slight that may be. For example, youngsters will be trained to carry scissors in such a way as to minimize danger. Beyond this, where the welfare of the pupil is central to the values and ethos of the school, action may be taken to address wider issues. These may include sex education, anti-drugs education, anti-smoking education, anti-bullying policies, healthy eating education, environmental education, road safety, personal protection, education for sustainable development, whatever is currently of general concern.

Risk assessment

A hazard means anything that can cause harm, while risk is the chance that someone might get hurt. Risks can be high or low. Your task is to make sure that the precautions we take mean that the risk is small. Getting rid of some risks is an obvious choice. But making children's life entirely hazard free is not an option. Helping children to make the right choices about risk is part of our job. We need to expose children to hazards so that they can begin to make choices about risk for themselves. At the same time we need to make the risks as small as possible so as to avoid accidents. The law says we have to take reasonable precautions.

Usually, the younger the child, the higher the risk of harm. But at any age you'll have some children who are not very sensible about risk. You'll need to take especial care with them. Think too about the needs of children with disabilities. Looking carefully at hazards in the subjects you teach and in the space in which you work should be a regular part of your work. Think about the children and the degree of risk to which they should be exposed. You'll need to be especially careful when you take children away from school on visits. For out-of-school activities you will need to complete a risk assessment form.

There are five steps in risk assessment:

1. Look for hazards.
2. Decide who might be hurt and how.

3. Evaluate the risk to decide about precautions.
4. Record your findings.
5. Review your assessment at regular intervals or at end points for one-off events.

Links

Child protection
Discipline
Out-of-school learning opportunities
Purposeful working atmosphere

Strategies

- Know what hazards are associated with the subjects you teach.
- Know how to minimize the risks in the subject.
- Agree with the children what the safety rules for movement around the classroom and the school are.
- Teach safety rules.
- Reward children who behave safely.
- Be prepared to punish children who are frequently reckless (see *Discipline* entry for punishment strategies).
- Know the procedures for risk assessment in your school.
- Deal with accidents promptly. Make sure that you review what happened and take appropriate action to reduce the chance of a similar incident. Keep a written note, dated and signed.

On out-of-school activities:

- Undertake a preliminary visit that includes information you'll need for risk assessment that complies with school policy.
- Write a risk assessment and have this agreed with an appropriate member of staff.
- Inform parents and carers in writing about the benefits and possible risks in the activity; obtain written permission from them.
- Prepare children for the out-of-school activity by including suitable health and safety rules in your teaching.
- Ensure that a suitable number of adults are available, able to accompany and take responsibility for children.
- Make sure all accompanying adults are aware of and will apply the rules that you have set.
- Review the health and safety aspects of activities as part of your evaluation of the event.
- If any incidents occur, make a signed record of the sequence of events as soon as possible.

Further reading

Websites often offer the most up-to-date information on safety issues.

www.gov.uk/h_s_ev/index has general guidance on both educational Visits and risk assessment as this applies to England and Wales.

www.teachernet.gov.uk/wholeschool/healthandsafety/visit/ is essential reading for planning safe visits.

TDA reference

Q31.

Self-assessment by pupils

In many school policies on teaching and learning one of the aims is to enable children to become independent learners. Self-evaluation is one of the strategies which will contribute to this goal. Children can use the process recommended in the first section of this book, just as well as adults. It is probably not appropriate to use the forms, as shown in the examples, but the thinking process is powerful. Pupils can ask the following questions about their work, behaviour, motivation, etc:

- 'What do I want to improve?'
- 'What do I need to change?'
- 'How can I change that?'
- 'Did it work?'

This approach is closely aligned to the problem-solving processes and cognitive acceleration strategies currently being promoted. It is a proactive approach and powerful mechanism for bringing about change.

When you ask a child to reflect on the quality of the work or behaviour he/she has produced, and he/she can respond by recognizing its worth and the need for improvement, the child has made a step towards his/her own decision making. Once children articulate what it is they are having difficulty with, they often seek help from peers and resolve the problem before it reaches the teacher.

Links

Active learning
Independent learning
Motivation

Part One
Target-setting

Strategies

- Teach the steps of self-evaluation in appropriate classroom contexts.
- Allow pupils the opportunity to comment on their own work or behaviour.
- Encourage verbal/written reflection and suggested action.
- Allow pupils to target set in specific areas (e.g. learning tables, spelling, keeping a tidy desk, completing work).
- Introduce overt reflective discussion (possibly by showing how you carry it out).
- Allow children to seek peer help with problems.
- Get children to set targets and report back on them.

Development

One of the purposes of self-assessment is to reflect on what you know, but another part is to establish what you need to do. In truly proactive fashion, this will lead to target-setting and further self-assessment. This would be a powerful learning tool if children could manage the process for themselves. Muschamp and a team of teachers in 1991 established a self-assessment system in a range of primary school classrooms. Her account in Pollard (1996) indicates what a complex process this is if it is to be established as a school practice. First the children have to be taught how to look at their work in a critical but constructive fashion. The early work of Muschamp's team revealed that children were not clear about the purpose of set work and the criteria by which it is judged. Beyond teaching the children to reflect on the correctness and quality of the work, they then had to structure a procedure of discussion (teacher–pupil, pupil–pupil) to enable successful target-setting and self-assessment. By the end of a year they managed to tie this in to reporting to parents and carers which involved contribution from the children.

Concept maps are used by some teachers as a way of getting children to mind-map what they know about a topic. Concept maps, with the content filled in, can be a vehicle for setting targets, allowing children to see what they are expected to learn and identifying what they do not yet know.

Further reading

Muschamp, Y. (1996) 'Pupil self-assessment', in Pollard, A. (ed.) *Readings for Reflective Teaching in the Primary School*, London: Continuum.

TDA reference

Q28.

Skills and strategies

Much emphasis is placed on what children should know, but it is just as important that children know how to do things. This is recognized quite clearly in subjects such as art and physical education. How to do things (procedural knowledge) is just as important in other subjects too, for example, science, geography, English and even maths. When planning work for children it is important to have learning objectives which focus on developing skills and strategies. These might be practical skills, such as how to use a saw or a protractor, or they could be thinking skills, such as how to get started on a problem or how to evaluate a product. Time spent teaching strategy will be well rewarded, as children will be able to transfer many of the skills and strategies to new situations.

In England certain skills have been identified as key skills which need to be developed. These are: communication, application of number, information technology, working with others, improving own learning and performance and problem solving. Currently these are being examined in national qualifications in secondary schools (age 11–16 years). All formal post-16 education in England encompasses key skills. Secondary colleagues will be building on the strategies children have learned in primary schools.

Links

Communicating clearly
Communication about learning
Problem solving
Thinking skills

Strategies

- Identify and promote skills and strategies by making them the objective of the lesson.
- Monitor children's ability to apply their knowledge.
- Encourage discussions in class about how pupils worked things out and how they are going to carry out a task.

> **Further reading**

Further information about key skills can be found at www.dfes.gov.uk/keyskills

> **TDA reference**

Q28.

Social development

Learning to be a social being is extremely important. Erickson (1963), a developmental psychologist, gives a framework for understanding personal human development, suggesting the stages that lead to self-sufficiency in adolescence. He suggests the need for a safe and secure environment in order to develop trust. Part of social development is about gaining concepts about gender, ethnicity, morality, citizenship and culture. Social interactions develop alongside intellectual, linguistic and physical capacities.

The milestones in social development are:

- Babies take an interest in other babies at about six months, they smile and make noises at each other. By a year some turn taking can be seen.
- Between 12–24 months infants play in *parallel*, that is, they play alongside each other rather than together. They start to become aware of a world beyond themselves, engaging in the rules that govern social exchange, for example, turn taking in conversation, expressing empathy, 'Mummy sad', 'Daddy cross'.
- At three years *cooperative play* with turn taking starts. When playing the children start to know who to give in to and how to be in charge.
- Four years sees *associative play* with sharing play items. *Theory of mind*, being able to understand the position of someone else, is acquired. Fighting is a normal developmental happening, though the cause of disputes is often soon forgotten.
- Six year olds have more friends and enemies and play in bigger groups; fights and feuds are sorted out with less adult help.
- Seven to nine year olds work out how to 'do friendship'; getting to know what they need to do to be accepted as peers.
- In adolescence friends become as, or more, important than parents and carers for social support. Girls tell their best girlfriends lots of things that their parents and carers don't know. Often teenagers form large groups with a shared interest, e.g. music, football, clothes. Single-sex groups start to break down. Heterosexual couples become more common. By the end of adolescence each person often has a smaller group of both male and female friends.

The wider role of the teacher is clearly important in this aspect of child development. School provides a safe space outside the home where an understanding of the society can be explored. In your classroom some children need help in understanding their own behaviour, and that what they do affects others. You'll want to think about how you help to develop their ability to make and keep friends. The use of circle time is clearly one way to do this. The open discussion of issues, for example, teaching children to be assertive rather than aggressive, is an important contribution.

Links

Discipline
Emotional development
Intellectual development
Relationships with pupils
Research and its uses

Further reading

Erickson, E. H. (1963) *Childhood and Society*, New York: Norton.

Mosely, J. (1999) *More Quality Circle Time*, Cambridge: LDA.

Keenan, T. (2002) *An Introduction to Child Development*, London: Sage. Chapter 9 'Social development' is a useful introduction to some of the issues.

Smith, P. K., Cowie, H. and Blades, M. (2003) *Understanding Children's Development* (4th edn), Oxford: Blackwell. Part 2 provides the theoretical background to social development.

TDA reference

Q18.

Special educational needs

Some children with SEN will have *teaching assistants* to help them. It is still your job to differentiate your teaching, design and set the tasks. The teaching assistants may be able to help you do this more effectively because of their knowledge about and experience with the child. They may know about and select additional resources and generally make your learning outcomes realistic and achievable. Usually the children they support have exceptionally severe and, often, permanent learning difficulties. These may include intellectual impairment sometimes in combination with sensory or physical impairment. This may include sight, hearing and/or mobility difficulties.

Some children may have sensory or physical impairments which do not impede their learning ability. They may have a teaching assistant to help with the sensory or physical difficulty. You will be expected to take their needs into account in your teaching and to use the teaching assistant to do this. For example:

- A child with a sight impairment may need a print size of 24 or even 32 point plus a strong electric light to undertake the worksheet you are setting for the most able children in the class. The teaching assistant needs the worksheet in good time to prepare it.
- A child with a hearing impairment may need you to use an amplifier so that your speech can be heard. The teaching assistant will check that the child can hear you.
- Wheelchair users often require more space. The teaching assistant will help you to organize the rest of the class to give the space.

Use any extra help you can get. Ideally, this will be an efficient and experienced teaching assistant but don't rule out volunteers. Older children working with younger children, peer support, community helpers, all are tried and tested, and given the right set of circumstances, they work. Remember parents and carers can often support their own child and do so willingly and well.

The need to deal effectively with children with *emotional and behavioural difficulties* (EBD) is becoming more important. These children will have Individual Education Plans (IEPs) with short-term targets for behaviour, sometimes referred to as an Individual Behaviour Plan (IBP). This is often in the form of an agreed contract between the child, teachers and teaching assistants. The contract will start with an area where you and the child think progress can be made. It will set out exactly what the child needs to do in specific contexts, for example, the child is required to start work as soon as it is set and to finish a specified amount of work each day. There may be 'time out' strategies for when the child feels that he/she may be about to lose control. The child may go, with your permission, to another class for five minutes.

On the occasions when things go seriously wrong for the child with EBD, there should be an agreed system for getting additional support into the class quickly and without fuss. You may not leave the class, so send a reliable pupil or two to fetch another teacher. The support should be from a senior member of staff. You'll need support from more experienced staff to meet some challenging behaviours. Children with severe and persistent difficulties may get extra help from a teaching assistant.

The aim is always to keep focusing on achievable targets for the child. It is not the child but the acts that the child carries out which are offensive and unacceptable. It is the behaviour that can be changed. You'll need to use a graduated response to children with EBD. Recognize that they may need much more positive reinforcement than other children. You always need to have one more step in your repertoire to deal effectively with children with EBD.

Common terms and learning difficulties

Below are some of the terms you may need to know. This list is by no means complete. Your SENCO will help you with the less common and the more esoteric conditions that some children have. The 'health warning' is that it is not possible to generalize from the named conditions, the ways in which this will affect the individual child. Each child experiences and over-comes difficulties in his/her own way. While your SENCO will suggest ways that often work for many children, don't expect these to be fool-proof. You and your colleagues may have to work hard sometimes to spot what works for a particular child. It is a great feeling when this happens.

AD/HD *Attention Deficit/Hyperactivity Disorder* Usually there are three areas of behaviour – inattentiveness, implusivity and overactivity – that are barriers to learning. Some of these children need highly structured programmes to make progress in school. Each child with AD/HD will have an individual pattern of behaviour with different 'triggers' and responses dependent on a range of things – who the teacher is, the subject, the time of day, what happened just before the lesson, e.g. an exciting playtime, etc.

MLD *Mild Learning Difficulties/Moderate Learning Difficulties* There are a wide range of these. Many children may have difficulty with one or all the key skills. Some can learn well but they may need much more time and help than others in the same class. Others may have organizational difficul-ties, things like often being late, often with the wrong bits of kit, and getting lost. Many children develop excellent coping strategies and should be expected to develop into successful learners.

SLD *Specific Learning Difficulties (including dyslexia)* Some or all of the following may be seen in some children: difficulty in sequencing, difficulty with spelling, difficulty in remembering a sequence of sounds in words, difficulty in recall of item and number sequences, and poor handwriting. Usually, if well taught, these children will find learning paths and develop strategies that compensate for these barriers to learning.

Asperger's Syndrome This is part of the spectrum that is called autism. Pupils with this can do very well in school settings with appropriate support. In primary school they may have delayed speech, cognitive difficulties, problems with understanding and using social cues, and an absorbing interest. Over time some of these improve, especially where help is given to the child to develop coping strategies.

Dyspraxia Often described as clumsy, these children have difficulties in planning and carrying out skilled, non-habitual motor tasks in a correct sequence. It is sensible to allow children with dyspraxia extra time to complete tasks. They, like many other children in your class, need structured support with many motor tasks.

Links

Code of Practice
Differentiation
Inclusion
Learning styles
Monitoring pupils' learning
Recording individual progress
Research and its uses
Teaching in teams
Working with parents and carers, professionals and other adults

Strategies

How would you provide proof for 'yes' answers to these questions? Turn these into statements to use as targets.

- Do I make sure that all the children in my class take part in all subjects and all activities?
- Do I plan lessons to include all children's needs?
- Do all the children take part in all the lessons?
- Do I use different learning styles and teaching approaches? Do I for example, experiment with ways of presenting that don't need much skill in reading.
- Do tasks and activities allow different children to get to different outcomes?
- Do I allow children with SEN the extra time they need to learn the facts and knowledge needed, by setting other children more complex and demanding tasks. (But not tasks that require new facts or knowledge otherwise children with SEN never catch up.)
- Are all children encouraged both to reflect on their own ways of learning and assess what they have learned?

- Do I make sensible use of learning support staff, involving them in planning and preparation for the child?
- Are other adults encouraged to work with the children in my class?
- Do we celebrate the successes we have?
- Do I enjoy the challenge that children with SEN present?

Development

Other countries have their own policies about SEN. Some segregate children with SEN into specialized schools. This is what used to happen in England and Wales. Recently though, inclusion is on the agenda for schools. While inclusion is not just about SEN, it is true that it is far the largest area of concern for teachers, parents and carers and policy makers. The policy was made explicit in 1997 in a DfEE consultation document *Excellence for All Children: Meeting Special Educational Needs*. This was used as an opportunity to review aspects of the education of children and young people with barriers to learning. The key principles of early identification and appropriate intervention were made policy. It was a major review of principles established by the Warnock Report (DES, 1978) and included a revision of the Code of Practice (DfES, Education Act (1991) and Special Educational Needs and Disability Act (581/2001)). The policy means that the number of children with SEN to be included in mainstream schooling may increase. See the entry on the SEN *Code of Practice* (**CoP**) for England to gain an overview on the policy and practice.

Further reading

There are a great many books and websites and organizations with useful information on SEN as a whole and on most of the conditions associated with particular special needs. The following is a short list:

Garner, P. (2006) *Special Educational Needs*, London: Routledge.

Spooner, W. (2006) *The Special Educational Needs Handbook for Trainee Teachers, NQTs and Teaching Assistants*, London: David Fulton, NASEN.

Thomas, G. and Vaughan, M. (2004) *Inclusive Education: Readings and Reflections*, Maidenhead: Open University.

Websites (Note that there are many more than these):

See DfES webpages for the most up-to-date information about SEN.

www.disabilitysite.net Look here for information and useful links by following the links for disabled children and young people.

www.halcyon.com/marcs/sped.html North American site with many useful links.

www.ipsea.org.uk Independent advice for parents.

www.nasen.org.uk National Association of Special Educational Needs.

www.nbcs.org.uk This site for parents and carers of blind children is an excellent source of support for those who work in educational settings.

www.ndcs.org.uk This site for parents and carers of deaf children is an excellent source of support for those who work in educational settings.

www.teachernet.gov.uk follow links whole school > SEN.

TDA references

Q19, Q20.

Standardized tests

These are tests which have been trialled and matched to a norm. Like IQ (Intelligence Quotient) the norm is 100 and children's results are converted using a table. The table allows for the age of the child to be taken into account. The child does the test which is marked and a 'raw' score is generated. This is then 'converted' using a table to a 'standardized score'. If a younger child gains the same raw score as an older child, the younger child will get a higher standardized score. When scores or ages lie on the limits of the normal range, the test is considered to be a less reliable predictor of ability. Standardized tests can be used to compare groups in various locations as well as measuring the child against the norm in different years.

Links

Research and its uses
Summative assessment

Development

A standardized test can be useful in research because it gives a norm which can be used to establish a base line and then children can be re-tested with the knowledge that a similar test will give comparable results.

However, Croll (1996) offers a nice comparison between norm-referenced and the criterion-referenced assessments which have come into more common use for measuring children's performance. He indicates that it may not be easy to operate a pure criterion-referenced system when we have age-related expectations. Certainly, in the light of his comments, it is worth reflecting on how a criterion-referenced system is actually used in the National Curriculum.

Going a step further, Lindsay (1996), reviews the place of standardized IQ tests in school in the light of children's, the school's and society's needs.

Further reading

Croll, P. (1996) 'Norm and criterion referenced assessment', in Pollard, A. (ed.) *Readings for Reflective Teaching in the Primary School*, London: Continuum.

Lindsay, G. (1996) 'Assessment of the primary school child', in Pollard, A. (ed.) *Readings for Reflective Teaching in the Primary School*, London: Continuum.

NFER Nelson is a publisher of standardized tests at www.nfer-nelson.co.uk/

TDA references

Q11, Q26(a, b).

Subject knowledge

In teaching you need a good knowledge of the subjects you are going to teach plus knowledge of how to teach them (pedagogic knowledge). For example, knowing numbers to 10 is something we all know but once young children have learned the counting rhyme, 1, 2, 3, 4, 5, 6, 7, 8, 9, 10, what else do they need to know? They need to know about conservation of quantity, recognize the symbol, count using one-to-one correspondence, be able to name how many are in a set and know which numbers come before and after others. These are all aspects of knowing numbers to 10 and they all need to be taught. As a teacher there is a significant shift to be made from having personal knowledge to having words to successfully teach that knowledge and finding tasks to help children understand that knowledge.

If you are confident and knowledgeable about subjects you will provide correct information to pupils and you will be able to answer their questions. You will also convey a sense of structure and continuity in the work that you do with the children. You will be in a better position to challenge children's thinking and will be able to resolve their misconceptions. Enthusiasm for a subject is easily conveyed to children. Unfortunately the opposite can be true too.

There are some subjects which will be your strengths and the children you teach will benefit from your expertise. In those subjects where you are not so knowledgeable you will need to research the topics and prepare your medium- and short-term planning carefully. Within a school's staff you will often be able to find someone (such as the coordinator) who will be able to provide some support with your weaker subjects.

Links

Active learning
Independent learning
Medium-term planning
Research and its uses

Strategies

- Research areas you are not sure of so that you provide an accurate and true experience for children.
- Convey enthusiasm.
- Seek guidance when you need it.
- Inform yourself well on topics as you teach them.
- Find opportunities, such as courses and conferences, to strengthen your teaching.

Development

A depth of subject knowledge and a particular interest in a subject will enhance your teaching and will often prove a strong motivator for the children. Spontaneous questions will elicit knowledgeable responses from you. You may even provide additional and interesting explanations which you, from your knowledge base, see as connected information; things which another teacher will be unaware of. This allows you to extend children's thinking and is particularly stimulating for able children.

Teachers who have a good knowledge base in a subject are more likely to be relaxed about teaching the subject, enthusiastic about the subject and less likely to teach misconceptions.

Further reading

Teacher Training Resource Bank at www.ttrb.ac.uk
Wikipedia at en.wikipedia.org/wiki/Main_Page
Children's texts and secondary text books
National Curriculum documentation at www.nc.uk.net

TDA references

Q14, Q15.

Summative assessment

Summative assessments are those made to summarize performance. They tend to mark stages of progress through the education system. The main purpose of summative assessment is to identify the stage a child has reached at that point in time. When marked papers are returned, these may be used for formative assessment. English national tests' results are analysed and the results are sent to schools to inform about weaknesses in particular topics. Typical summative assessments are GCSE exams, Key Stage test results and GNVQ which are all national assessments. The Key Stage tests are analysed and a report is made on national performance. In this way summative assessment can be used in a formative way.

Within school, summative assessment might take the form of half-termly and end-of-year tests, end of topic assessments, end of year records to pass on to the next teacher, reports to parents and carers, or records of achievement.

Links

Formative assessment
Foundation stage
Primary National Strategy
Recording individual progress

Strategies

- Ensure ongoing records are kept which will inform you when you need to summarize a pupil's achievements.
- Provide an assessment to summarize what a pupil understands about a topic at this point in time.
- Consider the use of self-evaluation when judging what a pupil knows or does not know.
- Be familiar with national assessment requirements.

Development

Assessment is used for many different purposes and therefore it is important that you select a form of assessment which provides you with the information you need. For a good summary of the purposes and principles of assessment refer to Harlen et al. (1996: 264).

Further reading

Harlen, W., Gipps, C., Broadfoot, P. and Nuttall, D. (1996) 'Assessment purposes and principles', in Pollard, A. (ed.) *Readings for Reflective Teaching in the Primary School*, London: Continuum.

TDA references

Q12, Q13.

Sure Start

Sure Start is a British government initiative which:

> Brings together childcare, early education, health and family support services for families with children under 5 years old.
>
> Sure Start is the cornerstone of the Government's drive to tackle child poverty and social exclusion working with parents-to-be, parents/carers and children to promote the physical, intellectual and social development of babies and young children so that they can flourish at home and when they get to school.
>
> Sure Start brings together service providers – statutory like health, social services and early education, as well as voluntary, private and community organisations and parents themselves, to provide integrated services for young children and their families based on what local children need and parents want.
>
> (www.surestart.gov.uk/surestartservices/settings/introduction (accessed 9/2006))

Initially it has been set up in disadvantaged areas of Britain. It functions out of 'Sure Start Centres'. The Centres are places where young children and their parents and carers can go for support and advice. Many have nursery facilities, Often these are identified as Children's Centres. The British Government plans 2,500 centres by 2008.

Links

Emotional development
Foundation stage
Parents and carers
Physical development
Primary National Strategy
Social development

Further reading

www.surestart.gov.uk

TDA reference

Q3(a, b).

Target-setting

The purpose of target-setting is to have clear goals which focus learning. There are several layers of target-setting occurring in school. The teacher will have targets for whole-class learning (learning objectives) and for individuals. Target-setting for pupils could be part of a pupil self-evaluation system. Some target-setting for pupils is shared with parents and carers. It is particularly important that achievement of these targets is recognized. This can be difficult to organize at the end of the school year.

Target-setting for the teacher is part of your self-evaluation system and continuing professional development. A more formal target-setting for teachers can be met when participating in an appraisal system. Here the targets are usually set for a whole year.

Schools have targets too. These are shown in the School Improvement Plan. Many LAs set schools targets to achieve in Key Stage tests. These targets are part of the drive to raise standards in schools throughout the country (England). Inspections can result in 'actionable' comments which then become school targets.

Links

Monitoring pupils' learning
Summative assessment
Teachers' employment and conditions

Strategies

- Set clear objectives in long-, medium- and short-term planning and monitor pupils' achievement of them.
- Create time to set targets with individuals and time to follow them up.
- Encourage children to evaluate what they have done and what they need to do next.
- Be aware of national and local target-setting for your school. Match these to your class performance.
- Set targets for yourself about your teaching skills.

Development

Target-setting systems are time consuming to maintain, especially when targets are individualized. However, individual targets are an effective way of meeting the needs of individual pupils. As much of the work will take place in a child's own time, with individual targets it is worth getting the cooperation of the child in setting the target. They will also need to know how they can go about achieving the target. A well-known acronym for target setting is SMART which stands for, Specific, Measurable, Agreed, Realistic, Time, all qualities which good target-setting should include.

Muschamp (1991) provides a powerful account of setting up self-assessment and target-setting (see *Self-assessment*). It was clearly a worthwhile approach for the children involved. Her teachers felt that there were links between self-selected targets and becoming an independent learner.

Smith (2001) describes a process for successfully establishing target-setting. His five steps are: timelines, future-basing, templates, anchoring and affirmations.

A fundamental issue when running a target-setting system is to establish how you will monitor that the targets have been achieved. This needs planning into your medium- and short-term strategies. If you do not follow up the target-setting, the motivation will die and the system becomes non-effective. No matter how independently a child is able to work, you are part of the contract which is made when the target is set.

Further reading

Muschamp, Y. (1991) 'Pupil self-assessment', in Pollard, A. (ed.) *Readings for Reflective Teaching in the Primary School*, London: Continuum.

Smith, A. (2001) 'The strategies to accelerate learning in the classroom', in Banks, F. and Shelton Mayes, A. (eds.) *Early Professional Development for Teachers*, London: David Fulton/Open University.

TDA references

Q26(a, b), Q27, Q28.

Teachers' employment and conditions

In England and Wales these are reviewed annually. The pay structure is fixed by law. However, while there is some automatic annual progression, increasingly your employers, the governors, have scope for discretion. The school will have a policy document about pay and conditions. Your job description will say what your school expects from you and this should be reviewed and updated regularly. It will state both the generic roles you'll be expected to undertake and any specific tasks that are your responsibility. In England teachers work 195 days, five of these are training days. Hours are also specified, but there is a let-out clause on this as you have 'to discharge effectively your professional duties'. This means that most teachers work much more than a 36-hour week. Professional duties include teaching, preparation for teaching, marking and report writing. Who you will teach and which room you will teach in, will be decided by your line manager, who is often the headteacher.

Performance management means that you will continue to be a life-long learner. You'll be developing the professional portfolio you started pre-qualification. In England and Wales as a newly qualified teacher (NQT) you'll start your first post with some targets in your Career Entry Development Profile (CEDP). As there is always something more to understand as a teacher, targets will not be hard to find. Furthermore, in most education systems, the extra experience gained will boost income. This aspect of your career is managed over a two-year cycle.

Your work is under scrutiny all the time. At first this seems intimidating but you will soon become used to it. The results you get and how you teach will be inspected regularly. These judgements will be used in different ways, one of which is to plan for your development. In addition to the appraisal you get from your colleagues, there are local inspectors and Office for Standards in Education (Ofsted) inspectors, who visit schools as part of the local and national accountability and quality system for England. Judgements made about your work contribute to the judgements made about the school.

Links

Discipline
Expectations about pupils' learning
Research and its uses
Safety
Teaching in teams
Values and ethos
Working with parents and carers, professionals and other adults

Strategies

- Be ambitious about all those you teach – expect them to do well and to achieve.
- Be aware of the expectations your colleagues have about you, know what your professional responsibilities are and undertake these wholeheartedly.
- Before accepting employment, check that the pay and conditions are what you want, including arrangements for your support and further opportunities for Continuing Professional Development (CPD).
- Prepare thoroughly for all aspects of performance review.

- Set realistic targets for your own development, these should take account of those the school has as its focus.
- Choose CPD activities that can be used to develop your curriculum vitae (CV).

Development

Beyond pay and conditions you'll want to understand what teaching involves. An important part of your professional responsibilities is the expectations you have about pupils. As a teacher you are expected to want your pupils to do as well as they possibly can. This means that you won't accept anything less than the best from everyone. Their 'best' means working towards raising achievement in all aspects of learning. But it also means that you have to do this from a knowledge base that respects and deals with difference. How you treat your pupils and work with colleagues, support workers, parents and carers and everyone else will demonstrate your understanding of your responsibilities. You are expected to evaluate yourself as a teacher, to build on your strengths and improve on any weaknesses. You'll work within the rules that are laid down by statute. This is a great deal to take on. It doesn't all have to be learned at once but it does all have to be learned.

Further reading

Bubb, S. and Hoare, P. (2001) *Performance Management: Monitoring Teaching in the Primary School*, London: David Fulton. A comprehensive guide.

Cowley, S. (2003) *How to Survive your First Year in Teaching*, London: Continuum.

Moyles, J. and Robinson, G. (eds) (2002) *Beginning Teaching: Beginning Learning in Primary Education* (2nd edn), Buckingham: Open University.

www.teachernet.gov.uk has the most up to date information about employment for teachers in England.

TTA reference

Q3(a, b).

Teaching in teams

You are responsible for working with your teacher colleagues, who will expect you to share responsibility for the school curriculum in all sorts of ways. They will expect a professional commitment to joint planning and preparation. At first you will need colleagues' help to overcome some of the barriers to learning that some of the children in your class may have. More experienced colleagues will support target-setting for children who are very able. Your subject expertise means that colleagues expect you to take a lead working towards solutions for the school in this area of the curriculum. You have responsibilities for the welfare of the children in your class. You will be expected to report on anything you think is amiss. You will want to celebrate children's successes, sharing these with colleagues. In a leadership role you will be working with other adults in school, e.g. nursery staff, teaching assistants and volunteers, right from the start. Increasingly you will come into contact and work with other adults related to the welfare of children. You will become aware of the issues that face the school as a whole. The management group of more senior teachers will expect your support and understanding.

Links

Communication with parents
Teachers' employment and conditions
Working with parents and carers, professionals and other adults

Strategies

As a colleague:

- Know your personal qualities, work from your strengths, but address your weaknesses.
- Be prepared to be flexible; it's supportive to release your teaching assistant on occasions to help in another class, it's a help to take a few extra children sometimes, it's OK to change your mind when there is new information.
- Empathy – putting yourself in someone else's position, understanding not just the words but the emotions that lie underneath – is a real strength. In the staff room, at year group meetings, listen to what is meant, not just what is said.
- Be task involved. Judge yourself and others on what is done not by who does it. It is about doing your best and doing an honest job.
- Be assertive. For example, find a form of words to tell someone why you are annoyed, 'When you do . . ., I find there is a problem. Can we find a way to deal with this?'
- Accept thanks graciously.
- Keep a hold on your sense of humour. There are times when humour can really help, but not always!
- Develop your understanding of the structures within which your school works, how it is governed, the challenges and the plan that has been agreed with the governors to meet these.

- Attend meetings and read the notes that are sent round and the emails (even when these seem, at first, to make little sense).
- Listen, ask questions, take part in the staffroom banter and conversations. It is tempting to stay in your own classroom when you have a great deal to do but, if you want to really be a part of the school, get into the staffroom, get yourself known, and get to know colleagues. Beware though, of the staffroom cynics, often they are very attractive company, witty and sharp but their comments can lower morale.

Development

Being part of a team means that you will get support in your day-to-day work and in career planning. Your colleagues will suggest when you should take on additional responsibility. Fairly soon, perhaps in your second year as a teacher, you will want to think about this. A curriculum responsibility, or other leadership role within your school, is often the first move. Think too, about a wider role, working with parents and carers and volunteers, or being the teacher representative on the governing body, or moving into union or professional association work. Moving school to gain experience with a different team is another decision that you will want to make at some point.

Further reading

Cowley, S. (2003) *How to Survive Your First Year in Teaching*, London: Continuum.
Thody, A., Gray, B. and Bowden, D. (2004) *The Teacher's Survival Guide 2*, London: Continuum.

TDA references

Q6, Q20, Q21(b), Q32, Q33.

Thinking skills (including cognitive acceleration)

As technology develops, the needs of society are changing and access to information is easier. This has brought about a subtle change in education. The need now is to educate people to manage the new technologies, to be able to solve problems and make decisions. This has tipped the balance of skills and knowledge slightly more in the direction of skills, particularly problem solving and thinking skills. Also, in the effort to raise standards of pupil achievement in education, people are examining the ways in which children learn effectively, hoping this will unlock the door to learning. Research into thinking and cognitive acceleration is currently being utilized to create better learning environments for children. What is particularly exciting is that this work, once the domain of psychologists, is now being linked to practical classroom strategies with interesting results (Adey, 1988; Adhami et al., 1997; Smith, 2001).

Links

Able children
Active learning
Independent learners
Learning styles
Problem solving
Questioning
Target-setting

Strategies

- Discuss with children how they will go about a task.
- Promote problem-solving strategies.
- Get children to set targets.
- Make sure children are aware and understand the learning objective and how it is to be achieved.
- Get children to reflect on the mental strategies that they are using.
- Encourage articulation of how they are working things out.

Development

Reflecting on the way we think ourselves is often termed metacognition. Thinking skills have long been a subject for study, but two research projects at King's College, London University, continue to generate much interest. These are *Cognitive Acceleration in Science Education* (CASE) (Adey, 1988) and *Cognitive Acceleration in Mathematics Education* (CAME) (Adhami et al., 1997). Cognitive acceleration is a term used to describe a process which allows children to speed up their ability to learn. By teaching children to understand the way they work and to develop strategies for solving problems, it is believed children can learn more effectively and perform to a higher level. Results from both CASE and CAME, which are based on Piagetian problem solving, have been very promising. They show improvement and transfer to other subjects. Other projects, where students employ metacognitive techniques, are also currently popular. These techniques require the student to consciously consider what processes and strategies they are using when working at a task.

Smith (2001) discusses 'pole-bridging' which is about utilizing as much of the brain as possible when doing a task. This can be done by articulating aloud what you are doing as you do it (talk yourself through, take notes, reflect and hypothesize on the situation). The plenary of a lesson often involves a form of reflection on the lesson. Smith goes on to discuss recent research on how our brains work and how we can maximize the learning environment of the classroom by utilizing this knowledge.

Further reading

Adey, P. (1988) 'Cognitive acceleration: review and prospects', *International Journal of Science Education*, 10: 2, 121–34.

Adhami, M., Johnson, D. and Shayer, M. (1997) 'Does 'CAME' work?' Summary report on phase 2 of the cognitive acceleration in mathematics education, CAME, project' in *Proceedings of the Day Conference of the British Society for Research into Learning Mathematics*, Bristol, November 1997.

Smith, A. (2001) 'What the most recent brain research tells us about learning', in Banks, F. and Shelton Mayes, A. (eds) *Early Professional Development for Teachers*, London: David Fulton/Open University.

TDA reference

Q14.

Time management

Teaching is a demanding profession so it is very important that you manage your time well and as efficiently as possible. Not only do you need good time management for yourself but you also need to expect it from your pupils. As a teacher, it is very easy to take on more than you can possibly manage. It is better to give a polite but firm refusal when approached, than agree and then not have time to do the job well. Work out your limitations and stick to them. This is good time management and avoids you and everyone else getting stressed. On the same theme, it is important to create your own free space, away from school work. This should be a point in the evening when you stop work or a regular commitment to a leisure time activity.

One of the classic ways to manage time effectively is to get started promptly and to limit the time to achieve tasks. If, on the other hand, you give yourself an open-ended schedule you will probably use up all of your time.

Try to avoid duplication when writing planning documents. Use key words and bullet points in your planning. Plan ahead as much as possible so that you can have part of each day to yourself. Use previous plans and ideas from text books if they are appropriate. ICT systems are useful here. Try to be efficient in your record keeping too. Decide for what purposes you need to keep records and then select the relevant information. Have a system which culminates in useful information at the end of the year.

Much of the above applies to organizing the children in your class. They too need to learn good time management habits such as getting started promptly on tasks and knowing how long they have to expected completion. Make these expectations overt so that they learn to develop their work habits. Allow children to make judgements about work. For example, 'How long do you think you need to complete this?' and, 'How are you going to start this problem?' Children also appreciate reward for work well done and well managed. This might be stars, house points, treats, a chance of a free choice activity, extra playtime, etc.

Links

Expectations about pupils' learning
Independent learning
Long-term planning
Medium-term planning
Rewards
Teaching in teams
Working with parents and carers, professionals and other adults

Strategies

- Make overt references to starting and completing work (expectations).
- Plan as far ahead as possible.
- Allow personal space in each day.
- Reward yourself and pupils for work well managed.

Development

Pollard et al (1994) in their research on how pupils spend their time in the primary classroom, found that they were 'task engaged', organizing or waiting for the teacher 20 per cent of the time and distracted for 20 per cent of the time. Looked at another way, most primary children spent between 65–75 per cent on task and task related activity. The question the researchers were left with was, 'Whether this "on task" activity is educationally productive?'

Further reading

Pollard, A., Broadfoot, P., Croll, P., Osborn, M. and Abbott, D. (1994) 'Using classroom time', in Pollard, A. (ed.) *Readings for Reflective Teaching in the Primary School*, London: Continuum.

TDA reference

Q29.

Timing within lessons

Timing of a lesson is a blend of planning the right length tasks, teaching within your allotted time slot, having a sense of time passing during the lesson and switching or staying with tasks depending on whether the children are engaged in a task or not.

If you check the clock at regular intervals you will build up an awareness of the time passing. At the end of the lesson you can evaluate whether you remained on schedule. This depends on you estimating, and then writing on your lesson plan, how much time you anticipate using for each part of the lesson. You will begin to refine your medium-term planning to match the pace of the children you are teaching. Increasingly you will find that you are able to judge how long tasks will take and the level of the work that engages the children.

Do not be afraid to alter the timing of a lesson if things are going well or badly. It is best to move on if the children are restless and finding it difficult to pay attention. (Windy days, Friday afternoons and school entertainments are some of the 'attention challenges'!) It is also your decision to extend a piece of work if you think the children are having a meaningful learning experience.

Regularly running out of time alters the balance of the lesson and means the conclusion is neglected. This is a valuable part of the lesson which gives you an opportunity to re-focus children's attention on the learning objective(s). You also need to maintain a balance between listening and doing. Overly long introductions leave little time for children to practise and consolidate the ideas and thus remember them.

Links

Lesson plan structure
Pace
Time management

Strategies

- Review timing of tasks and adapt medium- and short-term planning.
- Enter anticipated length of teaching and tasks on your lesson plan.
- Ensure that all sections of a lesson are delivered.
- Consider the balance within the lesson between listening, responding and doing tasks.

TDA reference

Q25(a).

Transitions

Transitions are the parts of the lesson when pupils are moving from one activity to the next. This could be when the whole class are required to enter or leave the room, when they move to and from the carpet session to their plenary or group work, or when they individually finish a piece of work and are required to move to the next task. All these situations have the potential for some pupils to behave poorly and not get engaged in the next task. You need to be well organized, clear in your expectations and clear in your instructions, so that the pupils have no doubt what is expected of them. If they know what they are supposed to be doing this makes it easier to deal with situations where they are not following instructions, because they clearly know they are in the wrong. Classes and children will vary in their ability to move round the room with control. Ultimately you are aiming for an environment where pupils can move round the room in an orderly and purposeful manner without you 'policing the traffic'. This form of self-discipline needs to be encouraged and praised and opportunities offered for it to occur. In the beginning though, there will be a need to establish discipline, which needs to come through you.

When clearing away, have a specific location for pupils to go when finished. You may need to do more than this. For example, it is not enough to say, 'go to the carpet when you have cleared away your art things'. This clearing up could spread over a long period of time and the early finishers will get bored sitting on the carpet if there is nothing to do. Often children will hurry if they think they are missing some new activity, so you might read a story or set a puzzle while the last of the artists complete their task.

Links

Discipline
Explaining
Instruction
Timing within lessons

Strategies

- Ensure that pupils enter and leave the room in an orderly fashion.
- Make your expectations clear about where pupils should be at the start and finish of a task before allowing them to move away from the previous situation.
- Ensure resources are laid out or available prior to the lesson.
- Plan good extension tasks for the fast finishers.
- If pupils are going to finish at different times, make sure they know what they are to do as and . when they finish.
- Be prepared to start another activity which late finishers can join in when they complete their last task.
- If the class cannot move properly all at once, send them to tasks a group at a time.

Development

Initially managing transitions is about you having control of the class and creating an orderly environment, but it should develop from there into a situation where children want their classroom to have an atmosphere where they move around like purposeful adults and engage in tasks because they are meaningful. It should not be a place where they have to keep one eye on the teacher to see if he/she is watching them and feel they have to misbehave because the teacher's attention is elsewhere. You will be working towards self-discipline. You should be able to move towards this by giving the pupils who are capable, more opportunities to manage their work. On occasions peer pressure can be used in group tasks to get the pupils with less self-discipline to toe the line. Croll and Hastings (1996) and Moyles (1995) promote the establishment of rules in the classroom. Laslett and Smith (1998) are more direct in giving four rules of classroom management.

Further reading

Croll, P. and Hastings, N. (1996) *Effective Primary Teaching*, London: David Fulton.

Laslett, R. and Smith, C. (1998) 'Four rules of class management', in Pollard, A. (ed.) *Readings for Reflective Teaching in the Primary School*, London: Continuum.

Moyles, J. (1995) 'The classroom as a teaching and learning context', in Moyles, J. (ed.) *Beginning Teaching, Beginning Learning*, Buckingham: Open University.

TDA reference

Q25(a).

Values and ethos

Your values will be reflected in your professional role. You'll want all those you teach to succeed at the highest level. To do this you have to know and understand about yourself, those who you teach and the education system in which you work. This is a tall order, so start by examining your own values. What do you hold dear? How does this square with what the society in which you live expects from you? For example, if you think honesty is important, how does this match expectations of your family, community and the schools that you know? Being honest is not absolute; in part it is about knowing when to tell the truth and when it is right to keep silent. Moral judgements are not always easy to make, sometimes you just have to hope that you're doing the 'right thing'. What you do and say, in any given situation, will establish your values with the children. For example, a pupil who disrupts a lesson by throwing paint on the floor might be punished, but a child who accidentally spills paint would not. The distinctive atmosphere of justice and equity you establish will be recognized as your values in action and the ethos of your classroom.

Links

Bullying
Culture
Discipline
Emotional development
Equal opportunities
Ethnicity

Expectations about pupils' learning
Parents and carers
Purposeful working atmosphere
Relationships with pupils
Research and its uses
Social development
Teachers' employment and conditions

Strategies

Some principles to support the strategies you use:

- Know the range of social and emotional development that you're likely to meet with your pupils.
- Accept that you need to develop your pupils' sense about right and wrong.
- Respect and deal with similarities and differences in culture in families and society.
- Recognize the fact that some pupils have a different view of right and wrong to your own.
- In your class, be clear with yourself about what is acceptable behaviour and what is not.

In your relationships with pupils:

- Expect high standards of behaviour and work from everyone.
- Work systematically with them towards a shared idea about what this means (ethos), e.g. through discussion as a class, in pairs and groups, to arrive at definitions and examples of these in action.
- Recognize that being fair does not mean treating everyone in exactly the same way.
- Being approachable does not mean that the children are your friends.
- Being firm means being just in your dealing and recognizing that not everyone starts from the same place.
- Rewards and punishments may not be the same for all children.

Development

The moral and social development of learners needs to inform the decisions you make about the values you teach and the ethos you establish with your classes. The aim is always to be stretching pupils' ability to make the right choices. You'll want to develop a climate in which it is right to challenge the opinions of others, where acceptance of difference is normal and where ideas about social justice can be explored. This ethos of a strong but tolerant morality is not easy to establish. Your reputation with pupils for being fair has to be carefully built. Children expect you to be 'in charge' but they also expect you to respect and value their views and opinions, especially where these are at variance from accepted social norms.

Further reading

Fox, R. (2005) *Teaching and Learning: Lessons from Psychology*, Oxford: Blackwell.

Haydon, G. (1997) *Teaching About Values: A New Approach*, London: Cassell.

Mosely, J. (1996) *Quality Circle Time*, Cambridge: LDA.

Mosely, J. (1999) *More Quality Circle Time*, Cambridge: LDA (both these are 'how to' books with many ideas about developing values and ethos).

Moyles, J. (ed.) (1995) *Beginning Teaching: Beginning Learning in Primary Education*, Buckingham: Open University. Chapter 10 by Sylvia McNamara 'Let's co-operate! Developing children's social skills in the classroom' is very useful.

Moyles, J. and Robinson, G. (eds) (2002) *Beginning Teaching: Beginning Learning in Primary Education* (2nd edn), Buckingham: Open University.

www.circle-time.co.uk

TDA references

Q1, Q2.

Whole-class teaching

The Hay McBer Report (2000: 1.2.7) confirms that, 'what we saw effective teachers doing was a great deal of direct instruction to whole classes, interspersed with individual and small group work'. They comment on the high level of interaction between pupils and teacher. Whole-class teaching has to involve all the children in the class. It is important that the work is differentiated; you have to engage all the children. A wide ability range may test the teacher's ability to do this. Recognize that some children take much longer to learn what others learn with ease. You'll want to have some tasks that everyone does, some that differentiate, and some to challenge the quick finishers. You'll want to make best use of any teaching assistants. None of this is achieved without high levels of planning and preparation.

Links

Whole-class teaching may require thought about each of these:

Demonstration by the teacher
Differentiation
Discipline
Explaining

166   Primary Teacher's Handbook

Group work
Independent learning
Instruction
Learning styles
Pace
Questioning
Timing within lessons
Transitions
Working with parents and carers, professionals and other adults

Strategies

In whole-class teaching:

- Use a variety of teaching strategies.
- Teaching and learning activities must match learning outcomes.
- Use clear instructions, demonstrations, explanations and careful questioning.
- During the lesson find out what pupils know and understand.
- Use carefully chosen examples, case studies and other activities that allow pupils to explore their learning.
- Differentiate the work, for example, one approach is to have tasks that are different for the least and most able pupils and some that everyone does. It is important to meet the learning needs of each child in your class.

Development

Whole-class teaching only works if the relationships between you and those you teach is interactive. The interactions between you and the children have to be based on respect and trust. Whole-class teaching is at its best when learners are challenged to use higher order thinking. You'll want to use open-ended questions, asking pupils to explain their answers, relating your questions to their ability. You'll also want to keep your teaching fresh. For example, while for many of the whole-class lessons you may follow a similar pattern, from time to time surprise the class with a different format.

It is worth recognizing that while whole-class teaching is a popular method of teaching it is not universally regarded as successful. You'll note that effective teachers use individual and group work as well. You should read the entries on group work and on independent learning. Getting a balance of teaching and learning approaches that suit your class will be your aim.

Further reading

McBer Hay (2000) *Research into Teacher Effectiveness: A Model of Teacher Effectiveness*, London: DfEE. Summaries can also be found at www.teachernet.gov.uk/docbank/index.cfm?id=1487

Moyles, J. (ed.) (2007) *Beginning Teaching: Beginning Learning in Primary Education (3rd edn)*, Buckingham: Open University.

Muijs, D. and Reynolds, D. (2005) *Effective Teaching: Evidence and Practice (2nd edn)*, London: Paul Chapman.

TDA reference

Q25.

Working with parents and carers, professionals and other adults

Time was when the teacher went into a classroom, closed the door and got on with teaching. These days you can expect to share the responsibility for children's progress with other adults, for at least some of the time. You'll regularly work with teaching assistants (TAs). You'll have contact with information technology technicians (ICT), lunchtime supervisors, janitors, cleaners, maintenance workers and school office staff. These are just some of your co-workers.

In the classroom, teaching assistants will expect you to know what it is you want them to do. They will also expect you to respect their expertise. Some teaching assistants are trained and often they are very experienced staff. It is becoming much more usual for all assistants to have opportunities to gain qualifications and for there to be a career structure for them. ICT technicians have mastery over the systems in school. Often they know about suitable software and how to get children learning from ICT.

The teaching assistant should be your best ally. The relationship you have is going to be important to both of you. Often TAs are there to help you to work effectively with all the children by, for example, supporting the group of children for whom English is an additional language. Or they support children with SEN. In the nursery, the TA's expertise, for example, in setting up appropriate play, is something to be appreciated and encouraged. Your co-workers' relationships with children and parents and carers are just as professional as yours, but because their position is different they often have a different understanding about the children from yours. Their views can add to your knowledge and inform the decisions you make.

Some areas of your work are confidential; it is important to recognize that this can conflict with the open relationship you'll want to have with them.

Plan your teaching to make best use of the help available. Co-workers need to be involved all the time to make best use of teaching time. Beyond the nursery, in particular, think about what the assistant needs to do when you are teaching the whole class. What is their role when you are explaining something to the whole class or managing a question and answer session? This is something to consult them about.

Links

Teachers' employment and conditions
Teaching in teams

Strategies

As a colleague support co-workers by:

- Being clear about what you want them to do to support your teaching:
  - i make sure you make good use of their time;
  - ii both tell them about and write down the tasks to be done;
  - iii give them the materials for the tasks you set;
  - iv ask for feedback;
  - v remember to say, 'thank-you' for the support they give.
- Including them in planning, in monitoring and assessing the children they work with.
- Agreeing on the class routines and procedures, making sure that you all discipline the children in similar ways.
- Involving them in problem solving and decision making. Together analyse, think about possible solutions, decide on actions and evaluate these.
- Recognizing and respecting their expertise and knowledge.
- Meeting their training needs (as far as you are able).
- Allowing the chance for them to work on their own initiative.

Development

Who else is in school? There are also support roles from other agencies, social workers, educational psychologists, specialist teachers, nurses, doctors, dentists, examination invigilators, school bus drivers, cooks, the police, the list goes on and on. Many schools have volunteer helpers, parents and carers and people from the community, local firms and sports teams. All these people add an extra dimension to your work. In particular, you will want to work out how to make use of volunteers' time in a way that respects them. Give them tasks that are educationally important, for example, helping children master an aspect of writing using a computer or by listening to readers. They will need your knowledge to undertake these tasks effectively.

Thomas (1989) identified the following areas as having the potential to create problems. Role ambiguity, 'who is the teacher?', may be a problem for some, including the children. Unintentionally obstructing each other or duplication of tasks is something to be avoided. Clear job specifications, ways of working and conflict resolution strategies need to be in place to make best use of additional adults. The children need to know who does what. In the classroom, think about the talents that all the additional adults have and how to use these to best advantage.

Further reading

Thomas, G. (1989) 'The teacher and others in the classroom', in Cullingford. C. (ed.) *The Primary Teacher: The Role of the Educator and the Purpose of Primary Education*, London: Cassell.

www.everychildmatters.gov.uk is another useful site.

www.teachernet.gov.uk has workplace reform with the duties of teachers and teaching assistants clearly set out.

TDA references

Q21(b), Q32, Q33.

Appendix: Mapping professional standards for teachers in England

Primary	Standards for QTS up to 2007 (DfES/TTA, 2002)	The Professional Standards Framework for Teachers in England for QTS from 2007 (TDA, Jan 2007 Draft)
Introduction		
Part 1 The self-evaluation process		Q7(a, b), Q8, Q9, Q29
Part 2 A–Z of effective teaching strategies		
Able children	3.2.4, 3.3.4	Q15, Q16
Active learning	1.2, 3.3.3	Q10
Assessment (See Feedback, Formative assessment, Summative assessment, Self-assessment by pupils)		
Behaviour (Discipline)		
Bullying	3.3.14	Q3(a, b), Q18, Q21(a, b), Q30, Q31
Challenge (Expectations about pupils' learning)		
Child development		Q18
Child protection	1.8	Q21(a, b)
Code of Practice	2.6	Q19, Q20
Communicating clearly	3.2.7	Q4
Communication about learning	3.2.7	Q4
Communication with parents and carers	1.4, 3.2.7	Q4
Competition		
Connexions		
Creativity		Q10, Q19
Culture	1.1, 1.2, 2.4, 3.3.6	Q18

Appendix: continued

Primary	Standards for QTS up to 2007 (DfES/TTA, 2002)	The Professional Standards Framework for Teachers in England for QTS from 2007 (TDA, Jan 2007 Draft)
Demonstration by the teacher		Q25(a)
Differentiation	3.3.4, 3.3.6	Q19
Discipline	2.7, 3.2.4, 3.3.9	Q10, Q30, Q31
Displays		Q25(a)
Emotional development	1.2, 2.4	Q18
English as an additional language	3.2.5, 3.3.5	Q18, Q19
Equal opportunities	3.3.14	Q18, Q19
Ethnicity	3.1.2, 3.3.6	Q19
Evaluating lessons		Q29
Expectations about pupils' learning (challenge)	3.1.1, 3.2.4	Q1, Q18, Q19
Explaining		Q25(c)
Feedback	3.2.2	Q12, Q27, Q28
Formative assessment (monitoring pupils' learning)	3.2.2	Q12, Q13, Q27, Q28
Foundation stage	3.2.1, 3.2.3	Q3(a) and (b)
Gender	3.3.14	Q18
Group work	3.3.3	Q25(a)
Harassment (Bullying)	Delete	
Homework and out-of-class work	3.3.12	Q24
Inclusion	3.1.2	Q1, Q2, Q10
Independent learning	3.3.3	Q19, Q24, Q25(d)
Instruction		Q25(c)
Intellectual development	2.4	Q18
Intervention		Q19, Q25(a)
Learning objectives	3.1.1, 3.1.2, 3.2.1, 3.3.3	Q22, Q26(b)
Learning styles		Q19
Lesson plan structure	3.1.2, 3.3.3, 3.3.7	Q25

Appendix: continued

Primary	Standards for QTS up to 2007 (DfES/TTA, 2002)	The Professional Standards Framework for Teachers in England for QTS from 2007 (TDA, Jan 2007 Draft)
Level descriptions		Q11, Q26(a)
Linguistic development	2.4	Q18
Listening and responding to pupils	1.2, 1.3	Q4, Q27, Q28
Literary, numeracy and ICT		Q16, Q17, Q23
Long-term planning	2.1, 3.1	Q14, Q15, Q22, Q26, Q29
Marking		Q26, Q27, Q28
Medium-term planning	3.1.2, 3.3.3	Q14, Q15, Q22, Q26, Q29
Misconceptions and remedies		Q28
Monitoring pupils' learning (Formative assessment)		
Motivation	3.3.3	Q10
Out-of-school learning opportunities	3.1.5	Q24, Q30
Pace	3.3.7	Q25(c, d)
Parents and carers		Q4, Q5
Physical development	2.4	Q18
Play and structured learning		Q3(a), Q10, Q15
Primary National Strategy		Q3(a)
Problem solving		Q25
Purposeful working atmosphere	2.7, 3.2.4, 3.3.8	Q30
Questioning	3.3.3	Q25(c)
Recording individual progress	3.2.7	Q27, Q28
Relationships with pupils	3.3.1	Q1, Q9, Q27, Q28
Research and its uses	1.7	Q7, Q8, Q9
Resources	3.3.1, 3.3.8	Q25(a)
Rewards		Q25, Q26
Safety		Q31
Self-assessment by pupils	3.2.2	Q28

Appendix: continued

Primary	Standards for QTS up to 2007 (DfES/TTA, 2002)	The Professional Standards Framework for Teachers in England for QTS from 2007 (TDA, Jan 2007 Draft)
Skills and strategies		Q28
Social development	2.4	Q18
Special educational needs	2.6, 3.2.4, 3.3.4	Q19, Q20
Standardized tests	3.2.3	Q11, Q26(a, b)
Subject knowledge	2.1	Q14, Q15
Summative assessment	3.2.2, 3.2.3	Q12, Q13
Sure Start		Q3(a, b)
Target setting	3.1	Q26(a, b), Q27, Q28
Teachers' employment and conditions	1.8	Q3(a, b)
Teaching in teams	1.5, 1.6, 3.1.4, 3.3.13	Q6, Q20, Q21(b), Q32, Q33
Thinking skills (including cognitive acceleration)	3.2.5	Q14
Time management	3.3.7	Q29
Timing within lessons	3.3.7	Q25(a)
Transitions		Q25(a)
Values and ethos		Q1, Q2
Whole class teaching		Q25
Working with parents and carers, professionals and other adults		Q21(b), Q32, Q33